Table of Contents

Introduction 3

Chapter 1: Instincts 6

Chapter 2: Composure 12

Chapter 3: Preparation 18

Chapter 4: Assertiveness 23

Chapter 5: Coachable 30

Chapter 6: Courage 35

Chapter 7: Authenticity 43

Chapter 8: Purpose 47

Chapter 9: Perseverance 52

Chapter 10: Communication 61

Chapter 11: Accountability 70

Chapter 12: Self-Care & Mental Health Wellness 79

Chapter 13: Integrity 87

Chapter 14: Be Bold 94

Chapter 15: Humility & Tolerance 99

Chapter 16: The Trio: 105

Chapter 17: Conflict Management 110

Chapter 18: Love & Support 118

Chapter 19: Positioning 124

Chapter 20: Be Fabulous 128

Acknowledgments 131

Conversations with Monica **133**

Introduction

Five years ago, I moved into a new home from a house that I lived in for a decade. That means it took what felt like forever to pack and unpack everything over the course of four weeks. This process allowed me time to do a long overdue purge and get rid of things I no longer needed.

A few months ago, my husband, Richard, was cleaning out the garage and asked about a box that I had stored in there. He was ready to throw it all out and I almost agreed. I thought if I had gone all those years and not needed anything from the box then surely it would be junk. Something pulled at my gut (I can't wait to talk about instincts later on!) and willed me to take the time to go through the box before I trashed it. I am glad I did.

At the bottom of the box was a cardstock-folded-beige booklet. It was stained with brown water spots and I could no longer distinguish the original color of the paper. Fortunately, all of the original hand-written information was still easily legible.

It was titled **"A Child's Campus: Progress Report; Grade 3 – K; 1977 – 1978."** Below the title was the following:
Student: Monica Saxby
Teacher: Mrs. L.V. Barnes
Director: Mrs. Ann Cooper

Well isn't this too cute? My pre-kindergarten three-year-old self was being evaluated. Wondering what she was like, I anxiously opened the booklet. Inside, was what you would expect in a report card – a lettering system designed to indicate my level of progress (G – Good; E – Excellent, and so forth). Nothing too remarkable of note, all Gs and Es, after all it was a pre-k-three class. I had coloring and counting down pat! However, I flipped over the last page of the booklet and there were the following written comments:

1. *Monica is doing well in class. She loves responsibility and participates in all class projects and activities. She came to*

class at a late date but has caught up with the rest of the class quite nicely.

2. *Monica is a great student. She is independent and likes to help others. She is a fast learner and a loving child.*
3. *Monica is working at a steady pace and is one of the best students in my class.*
4. *It has been a pleasure to work with Monica. She is very smart and well mannered. She is a special little girl.*

Well look at little "Miss Thing" showing off at the age of three! I was tickled pink reading who I was at three. What was powerful for me, was that there were a few things present about me that would serve as a good indicator of the adult I would become.

1. I was and am a leader. A full-blown woman leader.
2. I still like to help others. I have often had other women ask for mentoring or coaching to help them become better leaders. I hope this venue I have chosen does that for you if you are reading this book.
3. I am an executive in a high-paced professional work environment; a mother of two teenage boys, a wife, a daughter, a sister, a friend, a co-worker, a supervisor, an employee, a professional speaker and a writer. With all of those things, come great responsibility. I consider my path to be a journey of wins, losses, changes, adjustments, happiness, sadness, frustration, anger, and an assortment of other adjectives. However, with great responsibility comes the opportunity to in turn be responsible and share my experiences with those who may find it helpful so that you too can achieve whatever goals you desire.

I do not recall the exact moment that I was deemed a "leader." Not sure if there was a day I woke up and decided I was a leader, or if it was just the result of employment opportunities, I had over the last twenty-five years. Perhaps, it began at a Child's Campus at age three (By the way, this school is still in existence in the Flat Shoals/Glenwood area of Atlanta/Dekalb County GA, which is uber cool) or, if I became a leader just by default, being the first-born child out of three children. There is also the possibility that this started from the numerous times as a kid growing up in my neighborhood. My neighbor-friend-brother, Jeff Davis, and I were usually the captains of our self-made kickball teams.

I am unsure of the **_exact_** moment, but somewhere along the line it happened. I am not sure if I embraced it or if I grew into it. But what I **do know** is that I have learned a lot over my life and career that have helped me be a better leader, professional, mentor, and person. I will share those lessons with you here. It is my hope that when you are done with this journey with me, you will feel:

1. Empowered
2. Inspired
3. Motivated
4. Badass

Disclaimer Note
Dear Men,
While this book is geared towards my fellow *women* aspiring or developing leaders, there are many principles that are universal and applicable for women **_and_** men. You can join us if you like, just embrace the **#girlpower** moments that will pop up along the way.

Chapter 1: Instincts

Have you ever received an email at work that made your blood boil? So much so that you immediately and with fury start typing back your reply. You hit send and then have this small tug in the pit of your stomach. Although you were quite pleased with your ability to "clap back" at the individual who emailed you and caused this irate state you now find yourself in, something tells you maybe you should not have sent the email. You go to retract the email, too late though, the recipient has already opened it. Sigh. If only you had listened to the sometimes soft, but nagging inner voice that advised you to slowly step away from the keyboard!

My oldest son, Noah, had asthma as an infant and a toddler. I recall, quite vividly a horrifying night involving Noah about fourteen years ago. It had to be about 2am and I was in what is commonly known as REM sleep (I am a psychology nerd so some of that will creep in from time to time). REM sleep is described as the latter sleep stage where you are deeply sleeping, usually dreaming, and not as easily awaken by noises or other disturbances.

In spite of this, I woke up abruptly from my sleep somewhere around 1am to a sinking feeling in the pit of my stomach. I sat up in the bed alarmed, anxious and confused as to why I was startled. I sat motionless and silent for a few minutes. Nothing. Just silence and the faint sound of a police siren and a barking dog from several houses away.

Everything seemed usual, as I thought initially. I began to think that maybe I had a bad dream that woke me up. I took a deep breath, convinced that was why I woke up, even though I couldn't remember what I was dreaming about, or if I had dreamed at all. Then I heard it. The faint silence was no longer there. In its place was the clear sound of Noah wheezing and gasping for air from his bedroom. I jumped, almost tripping over an object on the floor and literally jolted to his room across the hall. He too was sitting up in his bed. When he saw me, his eyes widened and he grasped his chest with both of his tiny hands. He was two years old and having an asthma attack.

This story always comes to mind when I talk about why it is important for good leaders to have instincts. Not just having them, but knowing the role instincts play for leaders, and how to use them effectively. Everyone has instincts (or gut feelings) but women are uniquely positioned just by their genetic predisposition to be maternal or caregivers. I tell this story because while it is a personal story, in that moment I took on a leadership role. I had to make fast, precise decisions, while staying calm no matter how petrified I was on the inside. This was literally a life or death situation and I had to lead as a mother. That night ended in a trip to the emergency room and fortunately all was well in the end. He is still here, approaching seventeen years of age doing what teenagers do.

Noah is my first-born child and I had not considered myself to be "maternal."

It was around this time I began to pay more attention to the *super power* of **instincts** and began to apply it more purposefully in all aspects of my life, including my professional career. Amazing things started to happen as a result. I will conclude with what some of those outcomes were later in this chapter.

Let's put this in perspective for the workplace. If you are like the millions of other people around the world who use email daily as a primary way of communicating within the office, you have definitely seen your share of drama that results all because of an email conversation gone wrong!

Let's pretend your colleague at work, Joann, sends you an email. The email includes carbon copying to several people that you are unsure need to be in this communication in the first place and to top it off, Joann is saying things to you that feel accusatory as she is blaming you for an error that occurred on a project you are a part of. You are livid! First of all, you can't believe she is throwing you under the bus in front of an audience. (Why did Kelly, Mary, Tom, Lewis, Shelly, Amanda, Tonya, and David all need to be on this email?) Second of all, you believe this could have been handled in a one-on-one conversation. You are soo mad, you have lost your appetite and have canceled your lunch plans so you can "handle her."

You immediately begin to craft your email response, re-read it one time for editing purposes and click the "send" button as hard as your pointer finger can! Initially, you are quite pleased with yourself. You were able to "professionally clap back" at Joann and now she knows not to make this mistake again, right? Then it happens.

You re-read the email, all of it. You process what Joann sent and your response and there is a small tug in the pit of your stomach. Something tells you maybe you should **not** have sent the email. You realize that perhaps your response could be misconstrued and not place you in a good light. Crap.

You go to retract the email, too late though, the recipient has already opened it. By the end of the day, your boss wants to discuss with you the "situation" you and Joann seem to be having. Here we go.... if only you had listened to the sometimes soft, but nagging inner voice that advised you to slowly step away from the keyboard! ***Instinct.*** Effective leaders know how to use their instincts but it takes practice. Using your instincts and learning how to let it help guide some of your decisions, actions, strategic planning, interpersonal relationships, etc. requires three steps. I call these the three "T's"

1. Tap into it.
2. Test it.
3. Trust it.

Tapping into your instincts for me, means that you are finding the time to be still. You do not reflexively respond or react to a situation before you have had the time needed to reflect upon the situation. Many of us, including ME, get stuck here. A situation happens that we feel we must respond to because we are often focused on getting a task completed timely, or because just like the world and news seem to move at warp speed, so do WE. Taking a moment to critically think about a scenario before acting is becoming a lost art.

We have to get these back and good leaders understand this. If you revisit the example of the email exchange, instead of responding immediately, you wait just a minute or day (whatever is necessary) to respond, you give yourself the space to be still so you can hear what your instincts have to say on the matter. Trust me, your instincts, ALWAYS have two cents to offer. This is how you tap into it. Find the space to allow the inner voice to be heard.

Next you *test* what happens when you learn to incorporate your instincts into your decision making. This requires an <u>active awareness</u> of your instincts and focusing on the outcome. Hindsight is 20/20, we all know that. It is easy after the fact to say, "*I knew it!*" or "*I wish I had just gone with my gut in the first place*" or "*Something told me not to do this.*" Hindsight.

Imagine, if you will, how powerful it would be if you could actively use your instinct and connect it to the outcome? That is tapping into AND activating it. Here's an example, let's say you receive the same email above from Joann and because of the visceral response you experienced from it, you took some time to reflect on it and felt that it was best to reply with the following:

"I am confirming receipt of your email. I will reply back no later than noon tomorrow to respond to your concerns and questions. Thank you in advance for your patience."

You then follow this email up a few hours later with a more thought out response that was not a knee-jerk reaction. You hit the "send" button and feel good about your email with no regrets. You can now see the impact that taking the time to be still allowed. Proactively listening to what your instinct had to say and in turn, incorporating that into the other factors that are involved in decision making. Big difference from the email scenario I initially described at the earlier part of this chapter, right? Yes.

Once you become actively aware of how you tap into your instincts and begin testing, you will start to *trust* your instincts. We stumble here too. We talk ourselves out of a lot of stuff because we don't like what our instincts are telling us to do. We ignore the little nagging feeling because we have other plans. You responded to the original email situation upon receipt because you were just sick and tired of Joann sending you emails like she is the boss of you. You had enough of Joann and this was your moment to let Joann know it! When your instinct kicked in to say "Wait, I think I need to calm down first before replying," you decided you knew better and dismissed the warning your instincts tried to provide you with. Trust your instincts more. It is your internal alarm system. Sometimes you get a false alarm, but the majority of the time, the alarm is going off for a reason.

Learning how to master this as much as possible helps you be a **better** leader. The results are easy to see:
- You make better hiring decisions.
- You to play offense and not defense as much.
- You communicate with others better.
- You model for others how to manage adversity/conflict.
- You make decisions you don't regret.
- You avoid pitfalls of making hasty decisions.

These are just a few. I challenge you to use the three T's. Note your outcomes and what works or doesn't work for you. Everyone is different, but the fundamental concept here is universal. To be clear, I am not insinuating that instincts alone are all that is needed to make decisions. It is an important factor. But it is not the only factor.

Self-Reflection Challenge:
1. Identify a time when you made a decision based on your "gut feeling" and you did ***not*** regret it.
2. Identify a time when you made a decision that was **DIFFERENT** from what your "gut" was telling you. What was the outcome? What would you do differently in hindsight?
3. What helps **you** tap into your instincts?

4. How can you use your instincts to be more effective professionally?

Chapter 2: Composure

In October 2015, Secretary Hillary Clinton testified to the House Select Committee on Benghazi. Regardless of your political opinions, affiliations, personal regard for the Clintons or Hillary in particular, there were extremely notable lessons for women in leadership about the role composure plays in having credibility as a leader. This hearing lasted approximately eleven hours, starting at 10am ending at 9pm with breaks in between. This televised marathon event left me thinking: *if nothing else, this woman is giving us all a 101 class on composure.* She was grilled over and over about the unfortunate events that took place at Benghazi (google this if you want to know more about that). She handled the entire process with the type of composure that any woman can learn something from regardless of your politics.

Effective leaders understand that maintaining composure through adversity is critical. Women leaders understand that there are stereotypes about women that impact the way others perceive them. As a woman leader, people (men and other women as well) right out the gate, believe several fallacies about women in leadership:

- Women leaders are too emotional to lead important things.
- Women leaders will not make tough decisions because they can't handle the consequences.
- Women leaders aren't strong enough to stomach the grimy parts.

URGH. Infuriating. Let's clear up a few things here before we go further:
- Crying is not always a sign of weakness:
    - o Women cry. Men cry. Everyone cries.
- Yelling is not a sign of strength:
    - o Women yell. Men yell. Everyone yells.
- All black women are not angry (also sometimes noted as being *defensive*):

- o All races of women get angry sometimes. All races of men get angry sometimes. Everyone gets angry. Everyone can feel defensive.

Let's continue debunking these myths by being the phenomenal women leaders that we are. Back to learning...

I am sure if you are reading this, you have been in a meeting at work (formal or informal gathering of two or more people discussing a topic) and someone loses their composure. They may yell, cry, use profanity, slam a door, slam their hand on a table, abruptly stand up and walk away, raise their voice to the level right below a yell, roll their eyes, suck their teeth, cross their arms in defiance, or literally stomp their feet. Yes, I think that about covers it. When it happens in real time, it is either ridiculously funny, pathetic, or both to watch.

Observers of these types of outbursts often are stuck. They don't know what to do and sometimes they remain quiet and silent simply out of being shocked. At least that is what may happen the first time. If it becomes a pattern, the person loses credibility. People may not speak on it out loud, but something shifts around the person when the person acts in this way. Additionally, when the person acting out is the LEADER – we have a really big problem.

For obvious reasons, when the leader is unable to maintain composure, it is like an infectious disease. If unaddressed, the people that are on the leader's team will follow suit. They will begin to mimic this behavior. If the leader uses these tactics to make things happen, people will lose respect for the individual over time. This is akin to being on an airplane. Everyone looks to the flight attendants to see what their demeaner looks like. If they appear to be frightened, you better believe I am going to feel petrified. If the flight attendants are smiling and still passing out drinks and snacks, I'm going to think the turbulence I just felt must be minor because they seem composed.

There are a few key elements I think about when discussing the importance of composure. *Maintaining appropriate composure allows you to be heard more effectively*. No one listens to your message when you cannot convey it without escalating the conversation to an uncomfortable space.

Let's consider this example: You are a program director and lead a team of individuals at a community behavioral healthcare clinic. You must convey to them that you just received word that there will be a reduction in the budget, which means that tough decisions will be made about what programs will be funded and which ones will be reduced. Personally, you are angry about this news and feel as though cuts could have been made in other areas. Why *your* programs? The programs help people get access to healthcare for their behavioral health needs. Why make cuts where vulnerable people may be impacted? You completely disagree with the decision of the CEO, but you understand that the decision is final. You gather your team and begin with the following:

"Thanks everyone for being on time. I have some horrible news. I just learned that our department is losing forty-five percent of our funding. I can't believe this bullshit is happening. They expect me to figure out how to make adjustments for this loss. How?! How are WE supposed to make decisions about cutting funds from our program? We could never do that. It would be cruel. This is ridiculous, I swear. They don't really care about the people here; they just care about money. It's pretty obvious to me, not sure about you all. Anyway, we have to do what we have to do. I'll take a look at each of the programs, review budgets, and make some decisions about where to reduce funds. I'll let you know where I land. If you have questions, don't ask me because I don't know anything more than what I've just said."

While you cannot hear the volume of the voice, you can read the words and infer the tone. Is this the way leaders get messages across to their teams? Well, I am sure somewhere right now something very similar is actually happening, so yes, people do convey messages in this way. It's simply ineffective. The morale of the team was just depleted. The message being carried forth is tainted with the personal feelings of the leader and dismisses what may be true unfortunate realities of the economy at play. The leader is cultivating an environment of distrust, anger, and resentment. Maintaining composure is key in this scenario. Sure, it is probably personal for the employees and the leader. She may legitimately be heartbroken over the circumstances. However, effective leaders would understand how to rally the team together in crisis and not create discord. What if this is what happened instead?

"Thanks everyone for being on time. I know I called this meeting at the last minute, but we have some urgent news we need to discuss. This will be a tough conversation and we will have to pull together as a team to come out of this, but I believe we can do it. As you all know, our budgets depend on a variety of sources and circumstances. Unfortunately, due to the downward turn in the economy, one of our funders has dramatically reduced their allocations to our agency. As a result, we are being asked to take a critical look at all of our programs to determine where we can find some cost savings. In all, we are looking at a collective reduction of forty-five percent. I know that is hard to hear, I too had difficulty when I first heard this news. However, I believe we can use this opportunity to perhaps become more efficient and integrate some of our work. No matter what happens, we will do our absolute best to ensure that the people we serve are not adversely impacted. It may mean we have to do some outside the box thinking, but if any team can do that, it is ours. I will be meeting with you individually to review your programs and budgets. We will collaborate and come up with final recommendations."

Same message, different delivery and composure was maintained. It matters and has a huge impact on your ability to lead others.

Ultimately, this is about managing your temperament and emotions. It is an art. Some of us are good at it and some of us aren't. However, all of us can strive to be and do better on this one each day.

Lastly, maintaining composure allows **you** to listen better. If you listen to others, particularly in tense or adverse moments, you can often determine what is motivating them. I have often found that people can usually agree on the goal; it is the path or the process that people have the most conflict around. I'll talk more about this later in the book, but it's a good time to introduce the importance of this. Someone who has lost their composure will have difficulty hearing what others are saying.

Many of you reading this may engage in public events where you are speaking to large audiences. I have had the experience of speaking to very large, ballroom-sized groups to deliver a message. Sometimes the message was NOT what the audience wanted to hear. In turn, some of the questions/comments I would get from an audience member would be difficult. The questions would actually irritate me. This is fine and allowable, as I am human. What is not okay or effective, would be if my irritation impacted my ability to remain composed. Being in tune with my own feelings and temperament is critical in these types of scenarios. When I feel myself becoming agitated, I need to do something to proactively address it so I can remain composed.

A good example is "question management." What I mean by this is not allowing an audience member to derail the discussion or topic by introducing a question to me that is meant to distract, disrupt, or create chaos. If I receive a question such as this, (sometimes it is subtle and not very obvious) I respond with clarifying that some questions are best one-on-one and that I will be available for that after the meeting, or offer another option for that question. Otherwise, since you reading this are also human, your emotions will take over. Once that happens, the slippery slope to losing your composer **will** happen.

Looking for an example? Turn on any twenty-four-hour news network and you are bound to find at least three examples within one day of someone losing their composure because of their temperament and emotions around an issue.

Effective women leaders understand the role of composure, how to use it to gain credibility, and the pitfalls of ignoring this key critical leadership skill.

Now listen to this very **IMPORTANT** tip:
When you go home, or get in your car, or go behind the stage . . . **SCREAM**! Let it all out. Throw something or whatever it is you do to release. But in public or at the office, **be composed**.

Self-Reflection Challenge:
1. Think about a current event that helps illustrate what goes wrong when someone loses their composure in a leadership role.
   a. Analyze what happened (what was the cause, trigger, circumstance, people involved, etc.).
   b. Think about what could have been done differently.
   c. Think about how you felt when you watched or heard the scenario happen.
2. Identify a time that you lost your composure in a professional setting? What did you do that in hindsight, you would do differently?
3. Is there ever a benefit to losing your composure, from the perspective of a leader, in a professional setting?
4. Do you struggle with managing your temperament? If yes, how do you plan to work on this in order to be a more effective and powerful leader?

Chapter 3: Preparation

In a faraway place many moons ago, I was in a job that I felt like I was maxing out in terms of growth. I loved my place of employment, but felt restless. I knew I was about to come into a new season of something that was much bigger than the current role I was in.

I started to dust off my resume and slowly look at job opportunities outside of my agency. The employment opportunity that piqued my interest the most was a chief operating executive position in an organization that I had some familiarity with. There were pros and cons to the position. Location was the primary con, and of course it would be a change. Nobody ever likes change initially.

I remember that I reviewed the qualifications repeatedly before applying to **make sure** I was not overreaching. I questioned myself a little, wondering, if I was indeed ready to take on this type of executive position. After deciding that at a minimum, I did meet the advertised qualifications; I submitted my resume.

I received a follow-up call regarding my submission and landed the interview. Sweet! Validation that my restlessness was warranted and that it was indeed time for me to move into my new season. I was so excited that I was on my way to a new level in my career!

I interviewed multiple times with the CEO and other executives from the organization. I remember feeling good about my interview and feeling that I had done my best, which was all I could do. There was an extended time period between the interviews and receiving the news of the outcome. After a few follow-up conversations and the initial interviews, I was told that I was ***not*** selected for the position. Ouch.

Ok, I could accept that. Sometimes a position that you do not get isn't about just you. There are many factors that go into selecting candidates for a job. I understood this then, and have come to really understand it over time.

What I wasn't expecting to hear was that the reason I was not chosen was because the CEO felt that I was "not ready" to take on such a big role. Well alright. That stung a bit.

I was okay with not being selected but being told that I wasn't ready was something entirely different. I spent several days second guessing myself. Thinking, perhaps I had jumped the gun, and maybe I just wasn't quite prepared for the next level after all. I was completely deflated. I felt prepared. I felt ready. But from someone else's lens, I was not where I *thought* I was. At least this is what I believed at the time.

A few weeks passed and a new position became available that was much more complex in scope and responsibilities than the aforementioned position that I did not get. I thought, "well if I couldn't land the other job, why should I even THINK about this one." I continued to peek at the job posting until I eventually decided I was going for it. I submitted my resume and applied for the job.

The next day, I was contacted by the human resources officer at the company for an interview. I set up the interview for the same week and went into the interview with no expectations. The position would oversee child & adolescent behavioral health for the public sector for the state. It was a position that I knew I had spent years preparing for and although I was recently disappointed, it oddly made me stronger and more confident. I decided I would, again, do my best and whatever happened would happen. The day after my interview I was offered the job. Boom.

I tell you this story because it is a story of preparation on a macro level. Preparation means many different things but for this chapter, I want to spend the time connecting preparation and leadership. Reflecting back on my experience of rejection, only to in turn find what I was perfect for, taught me the importance of both resiliency and preparation. Leaders take advantage of every opportunity to learn something new, meet new people who offer different perspectives, study areas of interest in multiple ways, and take the time it takes to become knowledgeable or a subject matter expert. I landed the job that I did because I had done those things over time. I was prepared, but it didn't stop there. My story still continues, and I am constantly faced with preparation challenges.

Being prepared is not always only about studying information, going to school, taking special classes, etc. While these things may play a role, it is also the ability to anticipate what may happen as a result of your actions. What questions may come up based on what you are presenting or discussing? What's the strategy for addressing them? How do you account for and anticipate how different people with various backgrounds and perspectives may perceive your message? Is there someone I need to give a heads-up to about my actions, anticipating they may later need it? All of these questions are examples of how critical the skills of discernment and critical thinking are in the process of preparation.

This way of thinking about preparation is applicable across industries and a variety of scenarios. Preparation is a level of comfort that you have with the task at hand because you have garnered a variety of experiences and skills that back you up. <u>Prepared people are credible people</u>. Repeat that three times out loud. This is not about making mistakes (everyone does that) or knowing the answer to everything on the spot. It is more about being prepared for the expected and the unexpected within reason.
When I think back over my career thus far as a leader, I reflect on the "big deal moments."

These, for me, are the moments that I had to deliver complex information to large or critical audiences. People will often say to me they could appreciate the message, even if they didn't agree, because it was clear. Or they'd say something about me being relatable or articulate. Perhaps those are true things, but what has always helped me the most, was to just be prepared. Taking the time to critically understand the topic/subject matter; anticipating reactions, questions, or concerns; and being flexible enough to accommodate for what I did not foresee have been most valuable for me.

Preparation also takes patience. It takes some people years to get to the level they can already envision themselves in. They get frustrated because they are wondering why the job they want is not coming together, or their financial situation is not what they desire it to be, or fill in the blank with almost anything here. In most cases, you can point back to preparation. No one becomes an expert at anything over night. A jack of all trades literally *does* equate to a master of none. Success takes the amount of time it takes. It is different for everyone. What is the same for most, is that lack of preparation will almost certainly not lead to success, and you definitely will not be an effective leader.

No, I didn't get the job above, but it was not because I was not prepared; it turned out I was. Something else that I had been preparing for had to find its way to me. The first one was a misfire and not meant to be. That happens a lot. Don't get distracted by those occasional bumps in the road. Do focus on what your daily habits are that are preparing you to be an effective leader and a successful person, period. Practice those habits that lead to effective preparation. Over time you will see how critical something as simple as preparation is for effective leaders.

While this matters for both women and men, women have a great advantage with preparation. We are naturally good at it! We run households, plan parties, plan brunch, throw bridal and baby showers, host dinners, mange medical appointments, plan weddings, plan trips, and so forth. We prepare.

For years, I played fantasy football. I won two of the four seasons that I played, and placed second and third respectively the other seasons. The reason was because I studied the players, watched sports analysis, read predictions from fantasy sites, studied the moves of the other teams, anticipated what the opposition team of the week would do, and changed my line up accordingly. I was prepared. Similar to instincts, we have this skill already in our DNA. Getting used to deploying it and using it across your career is another thing. But it's there at our disposal, waiting on us to activate it. Preparation — another hidden super power that packs a mighty punch when used.

Self-Reflection Challenge:

1. Preparation comes down to three main ideas: Be knowledgeable, be flexible, and anticipate.
   a. Think about one of your primary career goals. Write down the ways you are preparing for goal achievement.
   b. Think about how you can ensure you are actively and frequently practicing what you wrote down to help achieve your goal.
2. As a leader preparation is critical. Think of a time when you were **not** prepared for a task and moved forward with it anyway.
   a. What was the outcome?
   b. How did you feel about it?
   c. What did you learn from the experience that has helped you now?
3. Over preparing is a real thing. There is a such thing as preparation overload (I made it up but it is a real thing, trust me!).
   a. What are your thoughts about how preparing too much can backfire?
   b. How do you personally find the right balance?

Chapter 4: Assertiveness

This is one of my favorite concepts to discuss. It is a sensitive one and I am going to be 100% real with you. I will give you a moment to get a refill on your glass of wine, cup of coffee, diet soda, or whatever you are sipping on because it's about to get interesting. Popcorn may also be useful here. I'll wait.

Assertive is defined by Merriam–Webster as *"disposed to or characterized by bold or confident statements and behavior."* Okay, that sounds simple enough and positive; what could possibly be challenging about a woman being characterized as assertive? LOTS OF THINGS apparently.

Over my career and personal life, I have been described as assertive and I agree with this characterization. This assertiveness means that I speak up on issues that I feel some type of way about, I assert my opinion, I am vocal about what I do **not** want and I will physically take the steps to achieve a goal. Isn't this how we are taught we should be if we want to achieve any form of success? Well, that's what my daddy always taught me, not sure about yours.

What I didn't count on until I experienced it, is like beauty, assertiveness is judged by the eye of the beholder. I think we can likely agree that passive leaders are ineffective leaders. In order to be a leader, you have to be assertive. Please do not get the following attributes confused with assertiveness:

1. Aggression
2. Defensiveness
3. Bullying

Assertiveness is a requirement if you want to be a leader, so why is this skill more complex when you peel back the layers? I'll tell you why — **Race, Gender, and Age**. All three of these attributes play a role in how others will perceive your assertiveness. As I am writing this chapter, I am managing a real time situation wherein I find that a skill (my assertiveness) that I have had my whole life, one that has made me into a woman leader, is a skill that has a double-edged sword.

On one hand, my assertiveness allows me to get stuff done. I am motivated by achievement and completion of a task. In order to achieve the things that I have wanted over time, I have had to assert in one way or another. I see this as a great asset. However, as I have become more seasoned, I also see that for others that view me, they may see it as: intimidating, aggressive, or ambitious. Unfortunately, I am not a club of one. Many women find themselves in the same conundrum: "How assertive can I or should I be to be accepted by others?" There is no easy answer for this, so let's explore more background first.

The Role of Race

I personally find it offensive when people say, "I don't see color, I just see people." I believe that when people say this, they don't mean to be offensive and probably *believe* what they are saying. It is an attempt to say all people are the same and that the color or race of an individual should have no bearing on anything that happens thereafter. It is a great sentiment that I believe is ideal but not realistic. It is okay to "see color" as that should serve as an early indicator that perhaps there are some cultural differences that you *need* to be aware of in order to respect the differences that DO exist between a variety of cultures, including race. The same is true in the reverse, I do see color and take into consideration the role of culture. That's what we are supposed to do, it isn't taboo!

Whether my audience is one or five hundred, people will see that I am black. My much-needed skill of assertion, to another black person, may look normal and familiar. That same level of assertiveness to a non-black person may look different. It may feel aggressive or even disrespectful. We cannot erase or ignore the hundreds of years that this country had legalized black slavery and the subsequent ongoing racial disparity that came during the civil rights era. There was a time when if a black woman looked a white woman or man in the eye, it was considered disrespectful. There was a time when asserting your opinion in any way that raised your voice by a single octave could have fatal consequences. The history is real and matters for the context.

Former First Lady Michelle Obama is a mom, highly educated, a successful professional, one of the most admired women in the country and *assertive*. She voiced her opinions with grace, intellect, and dignity while in the White House and afterwards. However, if you spent any amount of time on social media platforms when she was the First Lady or even now, you will find that there were countless numbers of individuals who saw her graceful assertiveness as "uppity," "angry," "unacceptable," "manly," "aggressive," and so forth. She was none of those things by my observations but unfortunately for some, this required skill set for any leader to have, was seen as a negative commodity on a black woman.

I have sat in meetings where I have definitely asserted an opinion or an action step. I have pushed back when I didn't agree with what was being decided by asking clarifying questions or "playing devil's advocate." I have seen the discomfort on some people's faces at my assertiveness. Sometimes it's a subtle non-verbal tell or a more aggressive response that lets me know my assertiveness is not appreciated. For me, finding the balance of the right dose of assertiveness comes down to a few concepts:

1. Understand that people DO see color. Decide if it may play a role based on the culture of the audience.
2. Take into consideration how people may perceive my assertiveness, plus my blackness, and make adjustments as required in order to achieve the end goal. In other words, I can adjust my assertiveness meter. I can dial back to a five if

needed to provide balance, or I can stay at a ten if that is also warranted.

3. Don't be uncomfortable using race and cultural differences to educate someone who sees assertion differently on a black woman. It doesn't have to be a dirty secret that can't be talked about. Teach one; lead one.

Gender and age have similar dynamics but not as convoluted as race. An assertive woman that is successful will make others uncomfortable, especially men that aren't used to it and other women who believe women should not be in certain roles. Women can be our best champions *or* worst critics. Don't assume just because the audience you may be dealing with is mostly women, that all women will see assertion the same. Some women don't like to see other women be assertive period, regardless of race. Let that marinate for a minute. You may need more wine at this point. Go ahead and refill; I'll be here when you get back.

The more women assert themselves into positions of power, the more you will also see that the naysayers aren't always men, or people of a different race. It can very much be other women, period. Women of baby boomer ages may have a set of principles that guide them to viewing assertive women differently than millennials may. It doesn't make either view wrong or right, but important to understand when working with cross-generational teams.

During the time period I was working on this chapter, Senator Kamala Harris announced her run for the Democratic nomination for the president of the United States of America. I took a break from writing this book to blog about my thoughts about it. While the blog entry covers more than the concept of assertiveness, it is a decent reflection to insert here while we are talking about this topic.

The Future is Female

I have been devoting most of my writing time to my book! This has cut into my blogging space. However, today I was inspired and took a break from the book writing to drop this blog.

I am ecstatic that Senator Kamala Harris is running for the Democratic nomination for the president of the United States of America! I am not as interested in using this platform for debating which candidate, from the ever-growing list "should be president" or should win the Democratic nomination. I am interested that a woman of color is stepping up and willing to lead in a time where true leadership gaps exist. I am very purposeful in being transparent about one of my missions which is to empower women around the world to LEAD. It takes guts, courage, perseverance, intelligence, and an armor of steel to step into politics as a woman, but even MORE so as a minority woman. The announcement by Senator Harris is a VERY big deal. Regardless of if you support her bid for the presidency or not, the power of her decision is notable by any standard.

It has only been a few hours since her official announcement and already the trolls have come out in force. I have seen the following themes:

1. Attacks on her ability to hold elected office (although she has done just that).
2. Questions raised about who she has slept with and if this is perhaps how she has become successful.
3. Outright racists comments by people that are emboldened to express such sentiments in the current environment we live in (and the courage the keyboard allows).
4. Questioning of her credentials.
5. People saying a woman can't win so basically why try. . . (pause while I look for something to throw across the room!).
My moment of pure joy was quickly tainted by the negativity I absorbed from reading the social media comments about her announcement. That only lasted a few minutes. Thank God.

I can't control any of that mess. Instead I choose to celebrate this moment Senator Harris has brought to us by embracing the boldness and audacity of stepping up to take a seat at the table for women of color. I choose to honor the collective whisper of our ancestors that have emboldened and empowered us for decades and centuries. I choose to embrace the strength of our black women ancestors who were raped, berated, beaten, broken down and made to believe they were the least valued humans. It is their DNA from which I was created and for which has empowered me. I choose to celebrate a heritage, on this Martin Luther King Jr. Day, that allows someone like Senator Kamala Harris to say, "I can and I will do more." I choose to thank her for daring to say, "I am running for president of the United States of America."

She will have tough days ahead for sure. I hope she is strengthened by the collective energy of every woman leader that has come before her, that paved a path for her to step up at this exact moment. Unapologetic courage, resiliency, confidence, intelligence, boldness, and ambition are all things that she embodies. It will be these same attributes that naysayers will use against her, as these attributes sometimes look different to the general population on a black woman. The significance of this moment, right now, at this time is not about the outcome. Kamala Harris winning the presidency is not what deserves a moment of reflection. It is the fact that she said, "If not me than who?" She took the leap. The power of this is incredible. If you can't see why this moment is soo significant, just stay tuned.

You can debate the politics of this announcement and decide if her platform is for you or not. I am not here for that, nor is this an endorsement. Today, I want to simply thank Senator Kamala Harris for this lesson on leadership. I want to honor this powerful moment and the message it sends to little brown and black girls across this country: You ARE a force to be reckoned with. You ARE powerful. You are Phenomenal. You are Extraordinary.
##

Assertiveness is an **absolute skill** required to be a good leader. However, becoming a great leader is being able to understand the impact race, gender and age may play in how your assertiveness is perceived. Assertiveness works effectively when you understand these concepts and can manage your assertiveness to successfully lead others.

Self-Reflection Challenge:

1. Do you consider yourself to be assertive? If yes, how do you think your assertiveness has helped you be a good leader?
    a. How has your assertiveness harmed your ability to be effective at times?
2. The race discussion and the impact on the perception of assertiveness is sensitive for some people. Do you think this is a real issue and if yes, in what way?
    a. Can you think of a time when race played a part in how your assertiveness was perceived (positively or negatively)?
3. Women not always being comfortable with other assertive women, regardless of race, was a concept I wish we had more time to dive into (We do in the live presentations though!) here. Do you think this is valid and if yes, have you ever experienced this?
4. If you do not feel that you are as assertive as you need to be in order to be effective, what do you plan to do in order to work on being more comfortable with this skill?
5. Do people sometimes see you as aggressive and you can't figure out why? What are some possible things that may give individuals this perception of you?

Chapter 5: Coachable

Before, I wrote this book, I developed a workshop with the same principles and title. I had no intention of writing a book at the time. I presented the workshop for the first time for an audience of about 65 people (including three men!). One of the audience members was a person who changed the course of my life.

I wrote the draft of the women's leadership workshop after deciding that I would prioritize the women's empowerment work about a year before it was finalized. At the time, I wasn't one hundred percent sure what my next move would be. I had a lot of balls in the air, an extremely busy career and not too much room for a new venture. At the end of the workshop, I was relieved it was over! I was nervous to unveil to others, mostly strangers, the leadership concepts that I had come up with. The work felt personal for me and I wasn't ready for it to be judged by anyone. *What if nobody found any of the information to be valuable? What if people laughed at me?* What if, what if, what if . . .

But I did it and guess what? Nobody threw peanuts or booed me off the stage. Instead, there was assurance in many forms that this work resonated with the majority positively.

One audience member in particular came to me afterwards and said something I will never forget. For privacy, I will change her name and we will call her Lisa. She asked, "Please tell me you have a book for this, yes? Why are you not on a stage?" She went on to give me positive feedback. This was crucial because Lisa is a professional speaker and one of the funniest people I have met! She told me the elements of the workshop that resonated with her and encouraged me to consider writing the book.

Initially, I resisted the idea of writing a book. I couldn't imagine when I would have the time, and it was beyond my initial plans. I already had what I thought to be good plans which included the development of the workshop and creation of a website. I felt **soo accomplished** about these steps and that seemed satisfying enough. Writing a book just didn't seem practical to me. Besides, I already had my own ideas and that seemed good enough to me.

However, I decided that besides the book writing, perhaps Lisa would have something else to offer by the way of advice. I set up some time to speak with her at a later date to get her input on my website and thoughts about speaking more. Lisa and I spoke for one hour. During that time, I wrote down multiple pages of notes and listened as she pointed out a million things that were all wrong with my website. She shredded it to pieces. *What?* I had spent a month working on the website and taught myself how to develop it. I was a genius! Besides, hadn't she already said I was awesome? Now I was confused.

I was slightly taken aback by her long list of criticism. But that only lasted for all of two seconds. I was eager to hear every word she had to say. The feedback, comments and criticism all made sense to me. I absorbed every single thing she had to say, swallowed my pride and decided to actually "LISTEN" to all of her feedback. Thank God for that, as she has gone on to become one of my primary go to coaches and the reason this book is now here.

Effective leaders understand that learning is lifelong, growing is a daily occurrence and excellence is always what we are in the pursuit of. Being open to being coached on what you don't know AND what you think you already know are critical. This means setting pride aside, listening to feedback and searching for meaning in things that you may not initially agree with.

Here's another example. Currently, one of my most admired women leaders in my life is my boss. I admired her from afar over a decade ago. I thought she was powerful, yet subtle, intelligent but not a know-it-all. I always knew that whatever came out of my mouth in her presence, needed to have value, offer something to the discussion and be <u>on point</u>. She was a faraway figure that I drew inspiration from, but she never knew it at the time. I watched in awe as her quiet yet powerful force dominated in whatever setting she was in.

As the universe often works, it links souls that are alike and need to be connected, even before you have a clue as to what is going on. This fearless lady eventually became my boss. When this happened, I thought, "Awesome, now I get to actually work with and for her, this is perfect!" What I didn't know was that she would use a variety of strategies to constantly push me to be better, go bigger and move out of my comfort zones. She sees me for who I am, observes who I can be and pushes me to embrace greatness even before I get there in my own head.

By the time you read this book, I will likely be forty-five years old (if the Lord is willing and the creek don't rise). As you may assume, at this point in time, I believe I know all that I need to know to be successful. Wrong. As an executive leader, I know that I have gained a plethora of experiences that have shaped me into an expert of sorts, hence what brought me to you all. However, it is critical for me to keep successful women leaders around me. I will never know everything there is to know about being a successful leader. I understand that for me, this is an ever-growing process and journey.

Being coachable allows me to be able to say, "Although I am coaching you right now, I personally need ongoing coaching because I will never, as one person, know everything there is to know." The minute I believe that there is no value in learning a new way, a new idea or absorbing any new information that helps me grow, I have failed as a leader.

As a leader, you must know how to step out of the coach role and into the player's role seamlessly. Every good leader knows that they will sometimes have to set their pride aside and be criticized without being offended. Effective leaders know how to be coached and allow it to happen. They actively look at each situation, conflict and everyday things in the world around them to challenge their own thinking. Effective leaders understand they have blind spots, and it often takes someone ELSE to point out those blind spots and encourage you to push through uncomfortable spaces in order to get to a better version of yourself. Great leaders take every opportunity to learn from others all around them.

Now to be clear, this isn't easy to do. Being willing to challenge your current thinking and expanding to a place that is beyond your comfort zone with the purpose of learning and growing is HARD, especially if it wasn't your idea! However, it is always worth it and it makes you better.

I have no desire to be surrounded by people who will only agree with me and not challenge my thinking. It is poor leadership to do so. Instead, I look for people with a variety of backgrounds, expertise and experiences to build a professional work team. If you are reading this, you are *coachable.* The moment you decide that you know everything you need to know and cannot accept constructive criticism; you have missed out on a critical lesson of leadership.

Don't focus on being the smartest and the always right, never wrong person. *Do* focus on being the person who is smart, sometimes right, and is always open to evolving, growing and learning more.

Self-Reflection Challenge:
1. How do you manage constructive feedback?
2. Was there ever a time you wish you had been more open to the concept of coaching?
3. If you find that you avoid being coached, why is that? Did this chapter make you think about being coachable differently? Why?

4. From your perspective, is it more important to you to be the coach of the team or be coachable?

Chapter 6: Courage

Recently on the news, there was a story of an elderly woman being home alone when an intruder entered her home. She got her shotgun and yelled out to the intruder that she was armed and if he made one more move, she would blow his brains out. Wowzers! The intruder fled and when interviewed by a news reporter, the would-be victim said something that rung true for me personally. She stated, "*I was afraid but brave.*" What a perfect way to capture how she reacted and felt in that moment; it instantly reminded me of an experience I had several years ago.

Atlanta was experiencing what we now refer back to as "Snowmaggeden." The city and surrounding metropolitan counties experienced a significant hit of snow and ice. The ice was the most problematic part and wreaked havoc on our already overcrowded roads, especially interstates. The mass exodus of early of students and government workers released early from Downtown Atlanta, plus everyone else leaving the city to try to get home, created a traffic nightmare. People reported being stranded in their cars on the interstates for upwards of eight or more hours. Cars were running out of gas, and hundreds or more cars were simply left abandoned.

I remember feeling "lucky" that I took heed of the warnings that started to come across the weather alerts and was able to be on the front end of leaving the downtown area to head home, approximately twenty minutes outside of the city.

I safely arrived to my youngest son, Micah's, elementary school and we made it home, avoiding all of the traffic problems I described above. Micah and I pulled up to our house, jumped out the car and were casually talking about the snow, school and whatever else you can get an eight-year-old to discuss.

We walked into the house from the car garage and immediately it felt cold, freezing cold, with a significant draft. From this point, everything always plays back in slow-motion for me in my mind when I have to retell this story. I noticed that the back door to the house was wide open. It had been kicked open aggressively because the door frame was completely broken, ripped from the wall. I froze. Fight or Flee?

Holding on to Micah's hand, I hurriedly shuffled him back to the car. Looking down at him, I could see the horror in his eyes as they mirrored my own. I put him back in the car, pulled the car out of the garage, parked it on the street and locked him in the car. I left the car, and went back into the house. Yes, I became the person you yell at when watching a horror movie! "Don't go back in the house!" But I did.

I simultaneously dialed 911 and kept them on the phone as I went through the house. The house had three levels, and I moved through each with fear and anger. I had no idea if the intruders were hiding somewhere in the house or not. It didn't stop me from continuing to search. The more I looked, the angrier I became. My house had been completely ransacked. All of it. I had never felt so violated and angry at the same time in my life. Fast forward, the home invaders were gone along with lots of items from my house.

After that incident, the reckless thieves attempted to return and take what they were unable to carry away the first time, twice. Two additional times they decided it was worth it to break into my house. Fortunately for them, or us, they were unsuccessful. The last attempt, I was home. To their shock and mine! I had overslept that morning and everything was thrown off schedule wise. I had just taken my shower and put on my last piece of clothing when I heard my doorbell ring. I KNEW exactly what was happening.

Ringing your doorbell was the first thing these robbers would do to see if you were actually in the home. Due to the time of morning, the fact that I knew I should have already been gone from the house, I immediately understood they were back. In a moment, I had to make a decision about what to do next. It wasn't rational in hindsight, but I ran down the stairs directly to the front door and in lieu of opening it, I yelled, "What the f*ck are you doing at my door!" I decided, in the moment, that if I sounded larger than life, fearless, and unhinged perhaps the shock value of that would push them back. It worked. Their plans were foiled.

About six months later, for a variety of reasons, this incident being a primary driver, I decided my children and I were moving. I had no clue how or to where, but I no longer felt safe and knew my number one job was to keep Noah and Micah safe. As you read in the introduction, we moved and this was the backstory. When I heard the elderly woman from the news say she was "afraid but brave, "I thought of course, because women are often put into scenarios where being strong is the only choice you have.
Being brave or finding courage to do something when you aren't sure of the how, but take the leap anyway, is a skill women have built into their DNA. When you compound this with the protective instincts most mothers innately have, you tap into another super power — **Courage**.

I share this story with you because it was a moment in time where I was pushed beyond my comfort zone in life, period. It was a time when I felt like either someone was going to hurt or kill me or my kids, or I would end up doing the same to whoever found their way back into our home with intentions that I would not wait on dissecting before I made a move. It changed who I was as a person. Made me more aware of my surroundings, more diligent about taking note of suspicious activities, made me a better mother and a better leader. I know what it's like to have the fear of God put into you and still find a way forward. I know what it's like to know I have to do this next step (in this instance move from a house I loved) and I have no idea how I am going to make it happen. I am sure you too can think of an incident where you were forced to find out how brave you could really be.

In the context of professional leadership, being a leader is <u>SCARY</u>! It means other people depend on you to lead the way forward. It means that you have to be accountable for the decisions you make *and* the consequences of the decisions. You have to inspire or motivate people to feel compelled to achieve the outcomes you want. You have to be able to handle some complex situations, including but not limited to people conflicts, multi-tasking high priorities, managing logistics, knowing enough of the details but able to see the vision and function on a macro level. WHEW! That is a lot, right? Yes, it is. This is not for the weak at heart. Courage is one of the most important skills to being an effective leader. While it is a critical skill, sometimes your experiences over your career or life make you stronger and in turn more courageous. Let me share a career experience with you that helped me become more courageous than I was about twenty years ago (and before my house break-in incident).

I spent many years working in a community behavioral health facility in the metro Atlanta area. I was first connected to this agency because I completed my graduate school internship/practicum with them. During the eight-month internship, I was pregnant with Noah, working full time at another agency and of course in school. I worked with individuals with severe and persistent mental health illnesses, primarily Schizophrenia. Additionally, it was also the year of 9/11. It was a busy and unsettling time for me personally and in our country. I found solace in the work that I did with the clients and can very easily remember the names of each of the fourteen individuals I spent the eight months with. The work was sometimes difficult but mostly rewarding, and I learned a lot that still informs me to this day.

After the completion of the internship and graduating from school, I wanted to continue working with the same population as a therapist. I felt connected to the work, I liked helping people who seemed to be the most vulnerable and I thought that I would be good at it. I had also spent some time working with children and adolescents in an inpatient/residential setting and would have been equally satisfied if my therapist role was with this population. What I knew for sure was that I was going to be a therapist. I applied to a few places but was happy when one of the call backs came from the agency, I completed my internship with. Sweeeeet. A place I was already familiar with and could easily slide back into the groove of things.

I completed the interview and got another call from them. The call was to offer me a job. SCORE!!! But wait, the offer was *not* for the therapist position that I applied and interviewed for. Instead, I was offered a manager position. *Manager*? I just got out of graduate school! I was sure there had been a mistake or a mix up with the applicants. No, there was not a mix up. The only person confused was me.

The interviewer's name (again for sake of privacy, I'll rename her) was Paula. Paula informed me that while yes, I interviewed for the therapist job, she believed I could handle a slightly bigger role. At the time, the agency was reopening, so to speak, a large child and adolescent treatment program. They had previously contracted this program out to another agency to run but had recently decided to bring it back in-house. They needed a manager to run the program. There would be a transition of some of the current staff; some would not be selected, and a large recruitment would have to happen to fill other vacancies. The program was expected to serve an average of one hundred youth a day with **intensive** behavioral health needs. Well that's not what I signed up for. I had a young baby (Noah was born by now) and honestly was looking forward to a less hectic life.

I was **scared** to take the job for all the reasons you can probably imagine. I didn't think I was experienced enough (I had zero management experience at this time), I had literally just completed graduate school, I had a baby and I was used to maybe managing fourteen clients at a time not one hundred clients **plus** about twenty staff! I was starting to question Paula's judgment! I also started to think, "these people must be desperate." I was all for challenges, but this felt like a set up!

I expressed my hesitation to Paula and she quickly talked me down from the ledge. She shared with me that she felt confident in my skills, including the ones I didn't know I had yet. Paula was confident, but I imagine this was not an easy sell as I was informed that the CEO of the organization wanted to interview me personally. I knew it! This idea of having me run a children's behavioral health day treatment program was nuts! The CEO must have agreed when he saw my management-less resume. I made it through that interview as well and in the process met someone who would become one of my favorite male mentors. He knows who he is and is probably reading this book beaming with pride (inset wink here). They really ended up offering me this job. As scared as I was about what I was about to embark on, I made the decision to go with it. Easily, in hindsight, one of the best decisions I have made, and the start of my leadership path. Paula and others believed in me, but it would have meant nothing if I hadn't had the courage to believe in myself.

Effective leaders have to be brave and have a level of courage that is not common for everyone. It would have been the easier path to accept another therapist position at that time as other opportunities did come up. The manager job was challenging and it was as hard as I thought it would be. However, I loved it. I loved the challenge, the kids, the families, the staff, our mission, and the hectic environment. Go figure. I did have the skills needed to be successful in the position and thrived beyond anything I imagined.

Leaders are often faced with making difficult decisions. In many cases, the decisions or actions require courage. You cannot be a scary leader. Who wants to follow that person? Nobody, is the answer. Courage should not be confused with recklessness. It just simply means that you are willing to do a few key things:

1. Take action when others do not want to.
2. Make decisions that are difficult and be able to own the outcomes.
3. Not being afraid of conflict. Understand that conflict always presents an opportunity to learn something.
4. Even when you can't see what is around the corner, be willing to prepare as best as you can and proceed to go around the corner in spite of your fears.
5. Have the ability to step outside of your comfort zone to allow space for growth.
6. Do not allow the fear of failure to be the loudest and most commanding voice. A little fear is okay; it reminds you that you are human. Being paralyzed or complacent because of fear is unproductive.

Courage looks different for women. It is sometimes subtle and quiet, other times not so much. Sometimes it is words and others it is the action, or a combination of both. Sometimes it's being the *only* woman at the decision-making table with all men and not being intimidated. Other times, it is being the only woman of color in charge of something large and high-profile, knowing that some people wish for you to fail and others will cheer you on whether you are up **or** down. Whatever courage looks like for you as a woman leader, know that you have to be brave in order to be effective and to reach goals that you never imagined you would do. Find your inner SHE-RO; name her and be her. Simple in concept, super effective in practice. (For the record, I am **always** channeling Wonder Woman) – Go forward fearless women and do good work.

Self-Reflection Challenge:
1. Do you think you have courage or is this a struggle area for you?
2. What does courage look like on you?
3. Think about a life event when you did something that pushed you to be braver than you thought you would be able to be.

How did that event impact your ability to be a courageous leader?

4. Do you believe it is possible to be an effective leader without courage? If yes, how? What does that look like for you?

Chapter 7: Authenticity

People are drawn to others who seem relatable. You see this play out in politics. It isn't always the most qualified person who sparks a movement or has huge mass appeal. It is often the person that others look at and feel they have some sense of a shared experience with. Often, people discount how important it is to be the best and <u>most true</u> version of yourself to be a good leader. But what happens when the person you authentically are is not what others are naturally drawn to? Well, this is a good time to insert an age-old proverb, *"Everything ain't for everybody"*!

Seriously, I get this question a lot and see it when I have help to mentor other women in particular. Women with strong personalities (present company included) are often deemed aggressive, scary, intimidating, unapproachable, and so forth. We may be praised for achieving the work outcomes or goals but asked to tap down on some of the personality components, something we don't see equally attributed to men. We touched on this earlier in the *Assertiveness* chapter, but this time I want to explore what happens when you attempt to **not** be who you truly are in order to fit into an environment you believe will be more willing to accept you — if only you were a little bit different. Or, if only you would just conform to what is comfortable for some, while others may be completely fine with who you already are.

The key principle when balancing the role of authenticity in an effective woman leader is the simple concept of **congruence**, which means agreement or harmony. When it comes to your core personality, if you are reading this book, chances are high that your personality is well-defined and formed and there is no changing that. Some women leaders will be criticized about how they come across to others, so in turn they attempt to make adjustments. You will perhaps see an adjustment in their behavior because of the feedback they received, but it will be short lived. Of course, this would be the outcome! You **cannot** change your personality to accommodate others' desires of who they think you *should* be or who they are more comfortable with. You are who you are. **Your challenge, however, is to balance being your true self while having the flexibility to have an adjusted version that meets the needs of different environments.** To achieve this, you need to understand how others perceive you. How would they describe who they think you are at your core? Is what others see congruent with who you believe you are?

I decided I wanted to test this. I literally just asked my husband to give me six words that he would use to describe my core personality traits. Here is his list:

1. Descriptive (e.g. I talk a lot; slight side-eye that this was the first thing out of his mouth!)
2. Loving/Caring
3. Intelligent
4. Assertive
5. Passionate
6. Optimistic

I then called my Dad and asked him the same thing; here is his list:

1. Intelligent
2. Thoughtful
3. Witty
4. Dedicated
5. Creative
6. Resolve (determined)

I picked these two people because one, they were both awake while I was writing this and were accessible. Second, because these are two people who should know me pretty well! I typed while they talked and put their descriptors in no particular order.

You will see similarities in their lists, and even what is different on the lists seem to be in the same ball park. I would say their assessment of who I am is congruent with who I think I am. I will not be able to stray from these attributes because they are my core personality. However, I am aware that *passionate, resolve, and assertive* **may** have to be dialed down a notch in some environments versus others. I can do this effectively because, as a leader, I understand that it is sometimes necessary in order to be effective.

I am always aware that this is who I am at my core and that my actions will reflect these core attributes in spite of what I try to do. I can be cognizant of the volume of the attributes and the impact it may have on the outcomes I may be trying to achieve as a leader. Finding the delicate balance in being true to who I am at all times (e.g. true to my core personality), while simultaneously adjusting to a comfortable level when necessary, is hard to navigate, but vital for success. Learning *how* to do this takes practice and is an art. Once you understand this, you will become a more effective leader.

When I work with women leaders on this topic, they struggle. The reason is because they cannot find the balance that allows them to be who they are and find a way to keenly adjust the volume of their characteristics that, if overdone, can be off putting. Their personalities are already formed, and it is insulting and offensive when someone doesn't like something about you. I mean, how much more personal can you get? You cannot help but be defensive, initially, because it is an attack on the core makeup of you. We tend to get stuck at that point.

We say things like, "Well, if they don't like me so what?" or "There's nothing wrong with my approach, there's something wrong with everybody else." Could those things be true? Yes, but could it also be true that if you want to be an effective leader, you start to take the time to figure out how others see you, how you see yourself, and find the path to being true to your core while adjusting the dial when necessary for the results you want? I say the latter is the way to go.

Looking for the sweet spot of a healthy balancing act for this, again, is hard. Some individuals go too far away from their core personality trying to be "different" and it fails. Anytime you are incongruent with your core self, you will be miserable and not authentic. Be you; be authentic all while understanding the art to all of this.

Take the time to understand who you are at your core. Embrace that person. It is YOU. Of equal importance, ask others how they see you. Is this the person you think you are, or do you see something different than what they do? With the exercise I did, in real time above, asking for input about how others see my core personality, I waited with baited breath while they provided their words! What if who they said I was differed from who I thought I was? Whew, it did not.

People can smell a fake a mile away. People also appreciate when you show them who you genuinely are. Doesn't mean they will like it, but people appreciate consistency in personalities; they know what to expect. Being authentic is a key ingredient to successful leadership, and learning the science and art behind it is where the hard work lies.

Self-Reflection Challenge:
1. Ask at least two people close to you to describe who they think you are at your core. This is the same exercise I did in the chapter. Is what was described to you congruent with what you would think? If no, why do you think that is?
2. Do you think being authentic is easy or difficult for you in a work environment? If yes, why is that? What can you take from this chapter and apply to help you?
3. The concept of dialing back or adjusting core personality attributes in order to be effective can be challenging for some. Do you do this effectively already and if no, why not?

Chapter 8: Purpose

"You can only become truly accomplished at something you love. Don't make money your goal. Instead, pursue the things you love doing, and then do them so well that people can't take their eyes off you."
— Maya Angelou

As I am writing this chapter, it is International Women's Day. I have loved seeing all the love and props being given to women in a variety of ways across social media. For me personally, I took it as a day to reflect on *my* purpose. I highly recommend you engage in this type of reflection often.

As excited as I am to write this book and sincerely hope that it helps someone become the leader they desire to be, I sometimes get overwhelmed with the process!

I experience writer's block on occasion and just finding the time to sit and be thoughtful in what I am writing and sharing with you is time-consuming. When I feel like this, I remember my purpose for doing all of this. My drive is *not* money, notoriety, or fame. I always imagine that this book will be read by me, my family and closest friends . . . and even then, I think most will flip through the pages to get to the bottom line because in the fast-paced world we live in, people do not like to read as much, at least those are my assumptions.

I am doing this because I feel as though my purpose is to continue to grow as a woman leader and make sure I bring other women leaders forward. I want to motivate others to be the best version of herself. That is my purpose for this work and for this book. I have to stay grounded in this purpose so that when things don't go as smoothly as I hoped, or I change course because a chapter isn't coming together the way I outlined, or because life is doing its thing and getting in the way of my process I can be grounded in "my why." I understand "my why" in a way that becomes clearer each day that passes. It feels amazing to feel as though I am living in my purpose.

Fourteen years ago, I was pregnant with Micah, my youngest son. I decided it was just as good a time as any to quit my job and become a stay-at-home mom. After about a month of not working outside of the house, I started to go nuts. I decided that I would open a business, and I did. It was a non-profit named **Serendipity**. I bought a book on how to incorporate as a non-profit for dummies, read it and moved forward.

I decided I would focus on providing counseling services for youth, families and eventually an after-school program for at risk youth. By this time in my career, I had a good bit of experience working with this population. I felt I understood enough about running programs to make this   logical step. Additionally, I had a lot of contacts that I could use to hopefully get the referrals needed to keep the business sustainable. As luck would have it, there was a perfect building and location available for lease that checked off all the boxes for a cozy counseling office plus an after-school program. I was able to acquire the building and proceeded with all the logistics for opening the business.

I was able to employee my mom as a receptionist and reached out to two former colleagues to see if they would be interested in contract work as therapists. One would focus on general mental health and the other on addiction. I also met a new colleague who was a psychologist. With her on board, I was able to land a contract with the Department for Juvenile Justice to provide psychological testing for their population. I had what I thought was a winning formula.

In the midst of all of these pieces falling in place, many things were also *not* going as planned. One of the clinicians that was contracted with me for addiction work, expressed wanting to have more of a managing-operating partnership in lieu of only being a contract therapist. We will call him Jason. I met with Jason and his wife for dinner to discuss the proposal and decided that it would be beneficial to have a partner. Jason and I agreed to move forward as partners, and he would buy into the business by paying an established dollar amount. Jason paid the money he agreed upon, and we began to make bigger plans on how to move the business forward. I was excited and he seemed to share the same sentiment. About a month or so after this partnership was established, Jason changed his mind and would **not** be able to continue as a partner and invest in the business. Initially hearing the news, I was disappointed, but that was only the beginning. Jason went on to ask for the money back that he had paid to buy into the business. Wait what?

A couple of key points here: For starters, the original purpose of the business was to be a non-profit. Once Jason came into the picture, a limited liability company was created and we moved away from the non-profit status. The starry-eyed plans I had for just wanting to help at risk youth began to be replaced by pursuing paths where I could have steady referrals; therefore, pursuing contracts took center stage. I underestimated the amount of money it would take for some of the start-up costs and the time to get certified for the after-school program. Oh, did you all remember that I was pregnant with Micah while all this was happening?

The original purpose was getting lost and now I was spending most of my time frustrated and overwhelmed. Eventually Jason and I ended up in litigation over the funds he paid me to be a partner and later reneged on our agreement. I also eventually (not right away) closed Serendipity for good.

When this was all transpiring, I felt a range of emotions from anger, sadness, defeat, frustration, you name it. As time passed, I saw it for what it actually was — a lesson that no school could have taught me. The real-life experience I gained from Serendipity was more valuable than any of the degrees I actually hold.

While there were MANY lessons learned from Serendipity, the biggest one for me was: *Always remember your purpose.* Do not be influenced by others whose purpose may not align with yours. Stand strong in your purpose and your walk and the experience will be different; it will be natural and it will be better. Serendipity had to happen in order for me to learn the value of this lesson regarding purpose. I never look back on Serendipity as a failure; instead, I look at it as the lesson it was intended to be.

Now when I have the opportunity to facilitate the Fab 30 workshops that accompany this book, I FEEL like I am in a zone; which for me, is synonymous with walking in your purpose. I feel confident, excited, comfortable, and happy. Sometimes I get advice from others (I am coachable remember) about this current path I am on. Sometimes the most well-meaning advice is not in congruence with what I feel my purpose is. I am cognizant of making sure that I do things at my own pace, in a way that is authentic for me and representative of what I know to be my purpose. You can only do that when you are confident about what exactly your purpose is. Know your purpose and stay grounded in it. Great leaders understand this makes them effective leaders and well-rounded people.

I started this chapter with my favorite quote by Maya Angelou. It has reigned supreme and has been a guiding star for my career and other adventures. I salute her on this International Women's Day and thank her for words of wisdom that remind you to not only find and follow your passion, but to know your purpose. When you find this sweet spot, everything else ALWAYS comes together. Always.

Self-Reflection Challenge:
1. Your purpose, in my opinion, can change over time. However, as you embark on different projects, experiences, or other things that you are leading, having purpose is key. This is often thought of as being purpose driven. Can you identify your general purpose in life right now? Take the time to list what you believe is on this list.
2. Are your actions in line with what you listed for number one? Are you walking in this purpose? If no, why not? What are

the barriers that are preventing you from doing so? How can you remove these barriers?

3. Have you embarked on a project or experience and realized you were not moving within your purpose? If yes, what did you learn from this and how did you exit it.

4. How do you think a leader who is *not* purpose driven leads?

5. What is the impact that you believe purpose driven leaders have on others around them?

Chapter 9: Perseverance

About fifteen years ago, I wrote an entire fiction book. This was out of the blue and without any real intention of doing so. I literally, one day, sat at my computer and started telling a story. I had an idea of the main story that I wanted to tell and drew inspiration for the primary characters from real-life. However, once I started writing the story, it took on a life of its own. I became completely consumed by the characters in the story, who morphed into their own beings, and moved far away from the real-life inspirations from which they were first born.

This book became all-consuming. Any free time I had; I was writing. In all, it took me a few months to finish the book.
A select few individuals got to read it in its entirety, but once it was done, that was it. I never completed my limited attempt to publish it or make it something more available for consumption for years.

There was a time where I did think, "I can and should self-publish the book." I got as far as doing some basic research and did get a book cover from a graphic designer. Then I stopped. Not because I didn't think the book was good, I think it was actually better than half of the books I was reading at the time. I didn't do it simply because I was afraid of rejection.

While I thought the story was intriguing, definitely cathartic for me, and worth a read, I didn't want the rejection of others not feeling it. I let that fear paralyze me and decided to just tuck the book away in a file on my computer to never be released. Besides, who did I think I was calling myself a "writer"? Don't you have to go to school for this or have a major publishing company backing you to consider yourself an actual author of a book? I settled with the idea that this was not something I could do.

Well, if you are reading this, you have quickly put together that somewhere along the line I must have decided that I **_do_** have the guts to call myself an actual author. After the first experience of book writing, I didn't imagine that I would necessarily revisit this, but yet here I am. When I developed the *Fab 30* leadership curriculum for workshops, I did not intend for it to turn into a book. Every time I was asked about this being a book, I quickly shut down the idea. In the back of my head, I had already decided that if I wrote an actual book, it would mean revisiting all the fears I had the last time. I didn't want to do that; I was comfortable with writing the workshop curriculum, comfortable with speaking with audiences and interacting with them, and comfortable with my knowledge level on the topic. See how many times I wrote "comfortable"?? Eventually, I realized that my workshops can't be everywhere; I am one person. However, if I wrote the book, the concepts I wanted to share with women leaders all over the world could spread. It was logical and I took the leap.

I sat down to begin writing multiple times. It did not initially come as easily as I thought it would. I had a task of translating a workshop, which has lots of interactions with live people and impromptu candid moments that are just not easily replicated, into a written format such as this. Nonetheless, I finally built up the courage to write and had writer's block before I typed the first sentence. Oh boy.

It was too late to turn back. I had already made the decision that this book was happening, so not seeing it through was not going to be an option. I had to get out of my own way and let the process just happen naturally. I began to look for writing inspiration and found it everywhere in different ways. My inspiration began to break down the writer's block and allow my creativity to have a place to flow to. I was able to free up the mental space I needed in order to be capable of getting in a writing space. This was wonderful and reaffirming in soo many ways. The sentences were turning into paragraphs and then into pages and finally completed chapters. I was fulfilling what felt like a purpose that I had run from before. I was completely committed to doing all the things I avoided the last time I wrote a book and was hyper focused on getting on the other side of this. I felt amazing.

Then life threw me a curve ball.

My dad was diagnosed with a rare form of blood cancer, Amyloidosis. In short, his disorder type causes the growth of irregular plasma cells from the bone marrow which in turn creates the formation of a protein that moves throughout your body and invades an organ. The severity of the disease is related to the particular organ the protein has "invaded." In my dad's case, the protein had set up shop in his kidney and heart. One of the worst places for the protein to travel to is the heart. If untreated, the protein will eventually cause the organ to fail. The course of treatment in his case is chemotherapy to slow down the development of the irregular plasma cells and the subsequent depositing of the protein into the organs. After chemo, he ultimately will need a stem cell transplant in his bone marrow. As I am writing this chapter, we are still in the middle of this battle, but we plan to win.

The news of my dad's cancer was a shock to my whole state of being. I went through all the emotions you can imagine mostly vacillating between anger, sadness, frustration, helplessness, and anger again. I stopped writing.

One day, while talking to my dad, he asked about my writing and how things were coming along. I told him how far I had gotten but that I was basically at a standstill. He started to ask to read a chapter every time I finished one so he could give me feedback. My energy was renewed. If me writing was going to give him something to look forward to, then dammit, I was going to write. I will write even on days that I am tired. I will write until I am completely finished and I will publish this book one way or another. In the midst of this, my dad sent me something he had written reflecting his feelings about what he was going through. I remember thinking that if he could write in the midst of his storm, I could push through and see this project to completion. I have been writing since.

Leaders will be faced with developing a plan or having a goal that they are responsible for seeing through. Along the way, we are often thrown curve balls and have to be able to find the will to keep going forward — *perseverance*. I shared the above personal experiences with you because those types of situations test your drive, your ability to stay with your purpose and sheer will. You learn something about yourself in the midst of storms as well as from the things you didn't see through to completion out of fear. Having the ability to do this is essential for effective leaders.

It is no accident that the chapter prior to this is about *purpose*. Once you have done all the soul-searching and self-reflection to determine what your purpose is, the second part is this: You have to be invested in your purpose in such a way that when it is not easy, or curve balls come, or life just happens in general, you keep pushing. You have to be soo sure of your purpose that when someone else tells you "no" (remember my earlier fear of rejection?) that it only fuels you to keep pushing. Why? Because you know what your purpose is, you will have the perseverance to see your purpose fulfilled. Every successful person that I know understands the importance of perseverance. They all have stories of failures and learning from them and being undeterred in moving forward until their mission was complete.

Leaders without this skill struggle to be effective. Who wants to follow someone who is confused when the plan needs to be changed for reasons they cannot control? Not many people that I know. Leaders should be able to effectively accommodate unplanned events that temporarily interfere with reaching the goal. Being able to adapt to the changing conditions and lead the team forward is a skill that not all leaders have. Usually, the disconnect I see is that the leader has not bought into the *"why"* part of they are doing this. They don't see the purpose and therefore cannot move or adapt when roadblocks appear. They are most likely to retreat versus re-grouping and pushing forward. Again, understanding the purpose and better yet, **YOUR** purpose, will lead to your ability to have perseverance in the eye of the storm.

We are about half way through this book, and this is where those of you that <u>truly desire</u> to be great women leaders will soar. If you have gotten the fundamentals so far and are willing to have the perseverance to see your goals achieved, then stay with me because you are in the right class.

As I have shared with you previously in the book, I blog in all this free time I have (insert nonstop laughter here!). I wrote the post below and would like to close out the chapter with it.

Houston, We Have a Problem!

May is mental health awareness month. I am glad there is a month dedicated to promoting mental health wellness, understanding mental illness and reducing the stigma. While I think there should be a daily effort to ensure you have a healthy mental health status, I appreciate the influx of interest in this topic if even for one month. In my blogs in the past, I have been pretty consistent in my approach around this discussion. I try to expand the discussion from what is sensationalized and often inaccurately portrayed regarding mental health in the media (e.g. movies, news outlets, etc.) to practical daily examples of how the functioning of your mental health status affects everything you do. People's default position in a dialogue about mental health is often, "Well I don't have schizophrenia, or bipolar disorder, or major depression, etc., so it doesn't impact me." I disagree, as there is much more to this dialogue. There are also many everyday reminders that we should use purposefully to manage our mental wellness.

Let me share a story with you.

Over the past several months, my dad has been dealing with a serious physical illness. He is preparing to move through a phase of treatment that will be a long, unpredictable and difficult road. I have been by his side throughout this process in ways that I never thought I would be faced with doing. I am a "daddy's girl" and he is everything to me. For as long as I can remember, he has always been my number one fan, always there for me and always has the answer to whatever problem I bring to him. He is smart, hip, very active and one of the few people that really get me. He is responsible for the woman I have become and has spent my whole life making sure that I knew I was badass.

Through his illness he has been strong, positive and everything that he would normally be in any difficult situation. I have seen him face many obstacles before and he ALWAYS comes out on top in the end. I expect this time to be no different.

As he/we entered the phase of treatment he is embarking on now, I developed a plan of how I could continue to be there for him like I have been for the past eight months. This time though, new complexities have been introduced to the situation and one of them is his treatment will now require out-of-town travel. For the record, I am a planner. I like things to have a logical flow that makes sense to me. I prefer order over chaos and my brain short-circuits when things fall outside of that. This situation with my dad is not allowing me to do any of those things! Instead I am forced to take it day by day, roll with the punches, and accept I am not in control of much here (Insert not so silent scream).

True to form, I just couldn't help myself (a serious intervention was totally needed at this point). I pulled out a calendar on one computer screen, had my meticulous notes about my dad's upcoming key dates on another screen, and my work calendar on a device in my hand. I began to plot out how I would take some time away from work to be there for my dad but still work (three days away two days in the office). I had to come back a second time and update that original plan because I forgot to account for my family (you know that whole wife and mom thing. . .). Sigh. Nonetheless, I now had a plan that allowed me to meet the needs of everyone. I'd be able to be with my dad for all the key dates and time periods, keep up with my office work, and of course still run a household. Boom. Who is the woman!?!? ME!

Wait, something was missing. I had not scheduled in a key activity. At what point, in between my well thought out plan, was I going to take care of MONICA? Hmmm. Great question and one that I had not considered in my perfect plan. I had been running on autopilot and tricked myself into thinking I could do it all. I realized, thankfully before it was too late, that I could not. This was okay. I accepted this. (I credit a very dear friend of mine who actually pointed out the flaws in my plan and nudged me to acceptance 😊.)

In order for me to be the best I can be for others who will need me, especially my dad, I need to not only make a list of things that need to be done when mom (me) is gone for spurts of time, or delegate work tasks for just a few days out of the week while simultaneously juggling critical tasks from my iPhone in between flights and doctor updates from a hospital . . . I needed to also make sure I was mentally ready and fit!
How the hell did I miss this? Better yet, how could I miss this? Trained professional here folks! Tsk tsk.

Fortunately, I caught it before it was too late. I noticed as the time was getting closer to the new treatment phase, I was edgier, more irritable, and ultimately a ball of constant anxiety after making my original plan. Yes, that faulty plan that excluded managing my own mental health wellness was a problem. Huge, big, jumbo, problem. Ultimately, my "plan" was scrapped and I decided to take a leave from my job for an extended period of time to focus and narrow my priorities and scope. Had I not done this; I would have fallen apart by the first week of this scary new journey.

I should know better. I should have done better in my planning. I am human and like many of us, I don't always prioritize management of my mental health wellness until I have already gone into full crisis mode and come completely undone. I speak about the importance of this, even train about it; but in my own crisis state, I had no plan for self-care management. And I was told wine could not be my coping plan. . . so there's that (I digress. . .). If I could be subject to this as a licensed clinical therapist, can't we all? YES. The answer is heck yes.

I shared this very personal story with you because it is my current reality and an example that mental health should matter to all of us because all of us are impacted not just during moments of unforeseen events, but on a daily basis. My challenge to you is that you start taking the time to add practices to your daily life that make management of your mental health wellness a routine "normal" thing that is embraced as a part of making you the best version of you that you can be. My challenge to myself is that over the next two months, I don't forget to practice what I preach. Later this month, I will circle back with some tips you can use to incorporate a proactive approach to managing your mental health wellness. After all, I will be utilizing A LOT of it in the upcoming months. At least for now, I am mentally prepared for battle. Let's go Joe, we got this!
##

Self-Reflection Challenge:
1. Is perseverance a strength you believe you already have? If no, what can you do to have the drive or will to see something through regardless of the curve balls?

2. How do you handle rejection (Perhaps not getting a promotion or hired for a job you interviewed for)? Do you keep going regardless, or do you tend to retreat?
3. Have you worked for or with someone that was a leader and was ineffective at completing projects or finalizing critical tasks? How did this make you feel?
4. Lack of perseverance impacts an individual's leadership style. If this is an area you struggle with, think about why you struggle with this. What are reasonable solutions you can put in place to help you develop this skill that are comfortable for you?
5. People sometimes conflate perseverance with aggression or assertiveness. I see perseverance differently from either of those. Perseverance for me, is the sheer will to see something through against adversity or curve balls. Think of a time when you demonstrated having perseverance in a situation. How did you take that experience and use it to help you be a more effective leader?

Chapter 10: Communication

I was recently preparing to facilitate the workshop that accompanies this book. While working on the slide deck, a phrase came to me that I swear came from the writing gods that sometimes whisper in my ear! The statement was "***Poor communication is the death of all good intentions.***" I repeated it out loud to my husband who was sitting nearby. He stated that for him, it was an "Ah-ha" moment and very powerful. Now, he repeats it often as he applies it to everything. (see men, you can join the party too)

When I coined the phrase, it was to illustrate that no matter what the intention of the individual, if the communication process is not effective, it will turn sour regardless of the original intent. This literally applies to everything! And while it is not the intent of this book, understanding this very well may save your marriage or personal relationship, but that is for a different book!

Ladies, this is one of the most critical concepts that determines long-term success as a leader. I have seen plenty of women not excel to higher leadership position that they have the intellect to excel but cannot because of their failure to master the art of communication. You can literally be the smartest, the most composed, an expert, well educated, and even the most dedicated worker. However, if you cannot get the concepts down in this chapter, none of those achievements or abilities will matter. You can have mastered every single concept in this book, but if you do not learn to master the art of communication, you will fail in the long-term. It is not a matter of if, but when.

Let's break communication down into two components: **Verbal & Written**.

Verbal: Tone and word selection are what people hear when you verbally communicate. Mixed into this equation, the person on the receiving end may have built in assumptions, biases or prejudices about you. You cannot control these extraneous variables but you *can* control how you choose to communicate knowing these elements are also factors in the communication process. I would say that now, with more experience, I have become much better at conveying a verbal message tactfully that may be difficult to receive to the parties involved. It does not mean that I always express what people want to hear. It does, however, mean that I express it professionally and I try to be clear. I have found that people often are okay with not agreeing with your position or what you may be attempting to persuade them to do if you can convey the "why" behind your message.

I recall a time on a job that I had just started. I was responsible for making a large policy change as it related to allocation of funding for contracted providers for the agency I worked with. It was a huge shift from the previous policies and would require a complete overhaul of the system in order to be successful. Our budget at the time was taking a huge negative hit (in the millions) and the intervention required was going to be complicated and needed to be quick and effective to stop the financial hemorrhaging. I will say more about this story later as it relates to accountability, so put a pin in the narrative as we will revisit it in the next chapter.

Once a plan was in place regarding the development of the new policy and the subsequent implementation and oversight, we needed a way to communicate this message to the intended audiences. The initial recommendation was to write and distribute a memo to the impacted individuals. At the time I was the new person on the block and I did not think this was the best way to communicate such complex information. I anticipated that the audience receiving this information would be surprised, frustrated and anxious. I knew it would not be a message or change that would be easily embraced. Because of these reasons, in addition to explaining the complex background that led to the policy change, a memo did not seem like the way to go.

I ultimately was responsible for the policy; so therefore, the final decision about communication would come from me. Or, let me say it this way — whatever the outcome was going to be, I would be the one held responsible. With this in mind, I made the decision to meet with the impacted providers in a face-to-face meeting. I remember, at the time, that my team members thought I had lost my whole entire mind. I am positive the belief was that I was simply clueless and that my naivety would be my downfall. I was willing to take the risk.

Within a month, the meeting was held. The audience was about three hundred people. I never second-guessed if standing up in front of this group was the right thing to do. I knew by the turnout, people were eager to listen, ask questions, and understand exactly what was happening and the potential impact on them.

I did not write out a speech. I had been knee-deep in the policy work for months, so I was very familiar with the details. I started my presentation by introducing myself and providing some background about who I was. I used information that would make me credible and relatable to the group. I went over some house rules. The latter was important. With an audience this size, it would only take one or two outspoken individuals to hijack the meeting. The rules were simple:

1. I have a lot of information to share, so please hold all questions until the end. I will stay as long as needed to answer all of the questions.
2. Be respectful in your questions and I will do the same.
3. One person, one question at a time. This isn't a press conference and we want to be respectful of everyone's time.

Simple enough. I went on to break down the heart of the discussion. I outlined for the audience the "why," the "how," and the "action steps." I was clear in my communication, direct in my responses and had a clear knowledge base of the information I was sharing. Most importantly, I was very mindful of my tone. Everything in the last two sentences is what you need to know when speaking for effective communication.

The meeting went fine and there was nothing thrown at me nor was I booed off the stage. In fact, people made a beeline after the meeting to talk to me individually. Not one single person out of the fifty or more people I spoke to individually had anything negative to say. They did not all like the policy change, (It would impact many financially as they would lose funding) but they understand the "why" and that I respected them enough to speak to them face-to-face. It was on this day, I learned how powerful face-to-face communication is and how important messaging and delivery really are from a leadership perspective.

This is both a skill that can be learned and an art that has to be acquired. Tone is an example of the art component. What many aspiring leaders miss is that you can say the exact right thing but saying it the wrong way will make the message no longer be right. **Take a moment to reread that last sentence and let it marinate a bit.**

The "in how" you verbally communicate is often MORE powerful and will make or break your communication if misconstrued. **<u>People cannot hear you if they cannot get past your tone (repeat 3 times)</u>**. If you sound condescending, dismissive, rude, mean, rigid, or disrespectful whatever you are saying will be heard through the cloud of the tone used. As a leader, if tone is a problem, how effective do you think you really are? Not as effective as you might believe. Sorry ladies, sometimes we have to put the truth all the way out there and let it just marinate into our souls! This is one of those times but don't worry; we are going to do this together.

This is tough because tone is also based on how you normally communicate because of your lifetime experiences and your genetic makeup. You are who you are! If you come from a family that communicates aggressively, you tend to do the same in other aspects of your life. If you come from a family where communication is passive or nonexistent, you will likely bring this with you into your career (and relationships). It's a part of who you are and what feels normal and natural to you. When interacting with others with very different communication styles from yours, conflict can occur simply based on miscommunication directly related to tone. It is very difficult being authentic to who you are as a person and striking the right balance of "tone art" in order to be a great communicator. Sometimes these things do not easily coincide with one another and have to be developed so you can be a better leader. I hear people say all the time, "Well this is just who I am; I am not changing for anybody." What I usually say back (for those I am rooting for) is, you simply have to find the art to balancing who you are, at your core, with how it gets expressed outwardly to achieve your goals. There is no one cookie-cutter solution because everyone is uniquely different. Each individual has to find their space to be authentically themselves and use that to help frame how they communicate.

I am often perceived as assertive and I am positive, depending on who is listening or watching, some will use the word aggressive. I am perceived by those that love me the most as being bossy. Hey, I am the oldest child of my sibling group, was an only child for five years, and I am the only girl. Lots of dynamics you can unpack there, but they all lead to . . . yes, I am bossy, assertive and unapologetic for it. I have however, figured out the art of communication from a leadership perspective that allows me to be authentic Monica but able to be heard regardless of a little sassy-ass-ness about me. I did not always know how to do this.

It isn't taught well. I learned it via exposure to bad and good examples. I learned how I did not want to be perceived and what was the most important component for effective communication from leaders — tone is the crux of it all.

Effective leaders understand their audience, scan the personalities and take note of perceived stereotypes or assumptions that may be made about them. A skilled leader understands how to use all of this information to deliver a message in a way that is:

1. Credible
2. Respectful
3. Fair/Reasonable

Now let's be clear, I am a mom with two teenage sons. <u>My tone changes accordingly</u>! I also am married to someone who has a similar temperament to mine, therefore I am more mindful of how I say things because I know how easily they could get misunderstood. Sometimes my sterner tone is <u>exactly</u> what I intended for it to be and I am okay with that. My hope for you is that you do some self-reflection and think about the role *your tone* plays in your communication style as a leader. I often find that people aren't always aware of this because they don't have true "gut checkers" around them who will check them when they need to be told they are doing something wrong. For these individuals, they have been able to successfully move through their careers because they have the skill set to do the job, but at some point, hit a ceiling and get stuck. They do not understand the reason they are not excelling is related to something as simple as "you just don't know how to talk to people!" Find out if you are this person ASAP! If you are, no worries. Hopefully by the time you are done with this book, (or attend a live workshop) you will master this art. I believe in you!

<u>Written</u>
I am a master of "word salad." I can out text and out write the best of them when I am pissed! My husband refuses to "text-argue" with me because I think he secretly knows I will win and that I won't stop until he concedes that he was wrong and I was right! What? I haven't mentioned I am competitive and like to win yet? If we are having a disagreement, I am very likely to sit on it, think about it when we are apart and then send him a text to express my position. Now, he will usually send me the same response:
"We *will talk about this when I see you later today.*"

What kind of foolery is this? Ha! He has outsmarted me. He will refuse to engage in a back-and-forth with me via text (He learned this through experience with me over the years). He got to this place because he felt that he did not convey adequately what he wanted to say via text because if I am already upset, I will apply a certain tone to his words that he did not intend. Well look at this — smart and handsome! He was absolutely right. We all do this. We read the text or email in the tone we perceive for the other person in the absence of their own voice.

In a professional setting, I swear this is where the majority of conflicts come from — poor email communication. I touched on this earlier on in the book for a different but similar concept. Again, similar to verbal communication, you can write all the best words, use perfect sentence structure, have no grammatical errors, be factually correct in the communication and STILL fail in being effective in the message if the tone is poor.

It is also easier for people to INTENTIONALLY use the exact tone they really mean in written communication versus verbal communication. Oh, the power of a keyboard . . . *see exhibit A: Any social media thread happening right now*.

It gives you a sense of power and courage that is not always present in verbal face-to-face communications. You can be a perfect verbal communicator and be a horrible written communicator. This will impact your ability to be an effective leader. I have been more upset over things in a professional environment that have been said to me via an email versus a face-to-face communication. People are simply emboldened, and all types of tact get left to the wayside when people are upset and begin to write.

I have read emails by individuals in leadership roles that have made me cringe. You know immediately that nothing good will come from it, and you sit back and wait for the storm of conflict to erupt. Great leaders take the time to make sure they are concerned about the quality of their communication no matter the form (verbal/written). There are easily applicable strategies for written communication that one can utilize today to get you started on perfecting this art:

1. Do not write emails when you are mad. Your tone will be angry and there will be no taking it back.
2. Ask someone you trust to be objective to read an email that you know may be sensitive BEFORE you hit send.
3. Be open to actually receiving the feedback from #2.
4.

There is soo much we can unpack in this chapter related to communication. This is the chapter/concept that garners the most energy and time in the workshops. There is such a vast amount of individual experience that make this discussion rich and transformative for many. I hope to see you live as this discussion never disappoints.

Bottom line, if you want to be an exceptional leader, do the self-reflection challenge below. Be intentional about being an effective leader. The world could use more of us right now.

Self-Reflection Challenge:
1. Ask five people that you interface with professionally about how they perceive you as it relates to your communication style. When you get the feedback consider the following:
a. Are their similarities across the feedback? Are there drastic differences, if yes, why do you think that is? (You may want to broaden your number beyond five.)
b) Is anything surprising about what you learned from the feedback? If yes, what was surprising or eye-opening?
c) Is there anything that you would be willing to change or do differently with your communication habits to make you more effective as a leader? If yes what are they? How difficult do you think changing or adjusting would be? How will you monitor success?
d) Are there things that were identified about your communication style/habits that you are unwilling to change, even if you know it is perceived as a negative about you? Why are you unwilling to change? Do you believe you can be successful long-term without implementing any change?
e) Do you believe any of the feedback you received was rooted in stereotypes or prejudices? If yes, what were they and how do you plan to use this information to be a more effective communicator?

2.   Repeat this same exercise but with people that are not connected to you professionally — family members, friends, associates. Just be sure the ones you select know you well!

3.   Without the feedback, from your own perspective, what would you list as strengths about your communication style/habits and weaknesses?

4.   Develop your own plan for how you will become a more effective communicator as a leader. Create the plan, implement the plan and monitor your growth. No one I have ever met has this down to a perfect science, so I feel safe in assuming we ALL could use ongoing development of this.

Chapter 11: Accountability

Remember the pin I asked you to stick in the story from the previous chapter (*I will say more about this story later as it relates to accountability, so put a pin in the narrative as we will revisit it in the next chapter . . .*)? Let's pick that back up for a minute here. I led you up to the meeting that took place and the outcome of the meeting with a focus on communication. What you could likely imagine is that there was lots of aftermath to such a huge, sweeping policy change. I always knew there would be pushback once we actually started implementation. I knew someone that "knew someone in high places" would pull that card. I knew someone would likely complain to those I reported to after the impact of the policy was realized. I went into this with open eyes about the outcomes and reactions. I knew that I would be held accountable if things fell apart and if what seemed like a good idea ultimately failed.

There was a period of time, in spite of the fact that I knew we were doing the right thing, it was becoming a headache as the complaints began to roll in. I stayed focused. I never thought the path we chose would be smooth sailing. I had to attend a couple of meetings with legislatures, contractors, and other stakeholders to explain the rationale to our policy change and answer a wide variety of questions. The vast majority were completely on board with the explanations and overall approach. But the few that were not, made their voices heard as well. It would have been easy for me to say, "Hey I am the new person here, what do I know?" Or looked to blame others on my team on the days when it was not all sunshine and glory.

I knew from the very start of the initial work that I would be the face of the sweeping policy change. I would fall or rise with it. Even though I worked with a talented team of people, it would ultimately be associated with me. I would be responsible for the outcome and accountable to all that it required me to be. I pushed through the not so great moments and stayed focused on the "why" and the expected outcome. We did successfully reach the desired outcome, alleviating the budget challenges that set this in motion within one fiscal year.

I realize that this story is told to you in an abstract fashion that leaves out many of the details. The lesson is not in those details that in reality was about eight months of work behind the scenes. The lesson is in the pivotal moments that can be told in this high-level reflection and categorized into these major lesson areas:

1. Communication
2. Perseverance
3. Courage
4. Instincts
5. Accountability

We have discussed one through four; let's focus on the fifth skill and lesson. It is one thing to be appointed, elected, assigned, designated, or hired into a leadership role. You think through the action of being in the "role" comes a level of responsibility that automatically makes you accountable. On the surface this is true. However, when actualized beyond the superficial surface, the fact is, true accountability is often *not* desired by the leader. When the leader does not accept the true level of accountability bestowed upon them by virtue of being in a "leadership" role, they are ineffective and do not thrive.

Effective leaders are accountable for the decisions they make and the actions of the team or group they are leading. They step up and accept responsibility for not just the wins but the losses and upsets. They do not only show up for victory laps and celebration parties, they show up to say, "We got it wrong this time, but here is how we are moving forward." They do not ridicule or demean others for making mistakes; instead, they support, coach, teach and uplift so the lessons can be learned. Effective leaders that understand what it means to be accountable do not look to others to blame. Instead, they look in the mirror to reflect inwardly on what happened and think about how to lead the next steps forward.

All of this requires making hard decisions at times. For example, it is easier to ignore someone's performance issues versus addressing the matter head-on. Addressing the performance issue may be uncomfortable and people have a tendency to avoid conflict not run towards it (most people). I look at this as an opportunity, not a conflict that should be avoided. I start from an initial place (staying with this example) of assuming that if it is someone I am working with and am responsible in any way for their outcomes, that I need to first determine what is it I can do to help this person be more successful. That is my usual starting point. I look for ways to support or coach because I see myself as being accountable for their outcomes, which is a direct reflection of me. Others, avoid addressing performance issues because they do not want to be accountable and want to avoid the conflict. No one benefits from this scenario. This is seen all too often when an individual remains in a position and they become known as "problematic." But, no one wants to be accountable for the role they have played in the scenario by allowing the situation to fester too long. Where was the leader in all of this? Usually right there, is the answer. The leader was unwilling to be accountable.

Another behavior that gets in the way of being a leader who is accountable is the inability to make a decision. I call this "flexibility gone wild!"

Being adaptable and flexible are great attributes for a leader, but when flexibility leads to permanently processing possible solutions and never making an actual decision, we have a problem! You see this in individuals in leadership roles that will kick the decision to someone else. It will often be disguised as needing guidance or clarity. In some instances, this may very well be the case. Sit that percentage of people aside. For the others, it is the discomfort that comes with being the leader that has to be accountable for a decision made. Nobody likes to be wrong or receive pushback from a decision gone bad. It never feels good so our natural instinct is to avoid this situation.

This should not be confused with a leader who openly solicits input from others for advice or is simply interested in various perspectives. No one person holds the monopoly on being the knowledge keeper of all things. Simply put, no one knows everything! So of course, a good leader knows this and utilizes other experts and seeks out the opinions of others to ensure the decision they ultimately will make is well- informed. This absolutely should be done and I strongly discourage decision making in isolation or only with people that think exactly like you do.

What I am talking about is when leaders collect information, get input from others, but will never make the decision. This is a good time to pause and ask yourself if you are one of these two types of leaders? Are you the leader who will never make a decision? Or, are you the leader who supports it by making the decisions that are kicked to you by another leader who is capable but unwilling to make the decision to avoid accountability? Which are you? If you say neither, great. But stick around because most of us that are guilty of this are not doing it knowingly all the time.

This is probably a good time to go grab a glass of wine, cup of tea or coffee and let this sink in for a second.

Most leaders who avoid making critical decisions, at the end of the day, do so to avoid being accountable. It may wear a different color lipstick, but in the end, it allows you to lead without having to do the hard parts. You know what happens over time to leaders like that? They do not thrive or excel and cannot figure out how others are surpassing them. This is a big reason why, and it's one of the biggest differences between leaders who are effective and leaders who are not. This is important for many reasons but it ultimately boils down to having the courage to be accountable. Making the hard choices, difficult decisions and owning whatever outcomes are associated with that. If this were easy, everyone would do it naturally! It, like most things that it takes to be an effective leader, is not easy and doesn't always come naturally. Being more aware of these characteristics and behaviors is the path to ultimately achieving the level of leadership you desire.

A final thought on the topic of accountability — you have to be willing to admit when you made a mistake or were simply just wrong. You will not make the correct call one hundred percent of the time. You will make some bad decisions and that is okay; that is not the point (same is true about life in general). The point is being able to accept this and being willing to learn from the process. Yes, this may also mean that there is someone that you strongly dislike . . . that you have to go back to and say, "I made a mistake." The ability to do this says more about your character than almost everything else I can think of. Effective leaders understand this, demonstrate it and coach others to master and overcome any fears they may have about what it means to truly be accountable.

The *lesson of failure* is intertwined so closely to this concept that I have condensed this for the purpose of this book into this chapter. It can stand alone as an independent chapter but flows so nicely here; let's touch on it now.

Being an effective leader takes courage as we have established. In addition to being courageous is the ability to take risks to reach the goals you set for yourself. I am confident that the biggest difference between hugely successful people and those that do not see the type of success they desire is simply Not being afraid to fail. They are not afraid to fail because the smartest people know there is always a lesson in failure. If you can brush yourself off from the bruised ego phase of failing at something, you can see all the lessons that are there to teach you what you will need the next time you try. Yes, there should always be a next time.

As a leader, you not only must be willing to take the risks, chances or seek the opportunity, but you also have the responsibility of role modeling for others what it looks like when you don't succeed and rallying the troops to continue moving forward and onward. I have learned that people are always watching you. They watch and learn from what you are good at and watch how you handle adversity. Understanding this helps you be more effective as a leader.
As a woman leader, we are constantly trying to meet so many different people's expectations. If you are a wife or a mom and a career woman, this pressure of not failing is even more intense.

I am on my second and last marriage. I was married previously for about eight years. From that marriage came my wonderful sons, Noah and Micah. It was not a bad marriage; it was simply one that I believe we both out grew. I was married at twenty-five years old and the person I grew into today is very different than twenty-five-year-old Monica. I knew long before we actually got separated and then eventually divorced, that we were not going to make it for the long haul. I remember the moment and I recall what I thought were legitimate efforts to work on the marriage because I didn't want to fail. My parents will be married for forty-five years in the fall, so I always grew up in a two-parent household and felt as though I had a good idea of what a marriage should look like. Well, what I know now is everyone's marriage is different and just because you have seen one example does not ensure you have seen THE example that is made for you.

Even though I had reservations about the sustainability of my marriage, other things played a role in why I lingered a bit longer than I probably should have, in hindsight. Ultimately, I didn't want to fail at something that significant. Even when it felt inevitable that the marriage would not survive, I didn't want to be considered a failure. You have to remember this was during the age range where all of my friends were also getting married and having babies. I would be the first of my immediate friend group to be divorced if I moved forward and while I am okay with being a trailblazer, this wasn't a first I wanted.

Ultimately, the separation happened and eventually the final divorce. While we initially separated, it was always clear that it wasn't a temporary thing. It was always understood that we were moving towards an official divorce, but for various unrelated reasons, that "official paperwork" process took longer to finalize than initially planned. During this time however, I considered myself to be divorced. That was how I spoke about it to others as the paper was a formality to me. My family and friends were supportive, did and said all the right things. But it still felt like I had failed. I also felt like the people who were trying to support me the most did not have the experience of what I was going through, so despite their best efforts — couldn't quite understand this lingering feeling of absolute failure.

I also had not quite prepared myself for how other people more distant from me, like co-workers, would now see me or treat me. If I couldn't hold a marriage together, how was I supposed to be a good leader? These were all real thoughts that I had and struggled with. I hated when people would ask me about my "husband" and I'd explain, "Oh we are going through a divorce." I would despise the sound of "aww" and sad pitiful pat on my shoulder they would give me. I didn't feel sad and definitely didn't want any pity. It would be infuriating. But they thought they were being helpful, so I would just nod and smile — anything to make them stop.

It took me a while, literally months, to stop thinking about the end of a marriage as a failure. I began to reframe what happened and took some time (a lot of time) to understand more about my behaviors and attitudes related to the relationship and use them as lessons for me moving forward. I reflected on what I now knew I didn't want in a relationship and who I needed to be in order to be a better partner.

Many, many years later and after a few bad dates and unsuccessful relationships, I married my current husband. There really was a "happily ever after!" I end up marrying the love of my whole entire life, but he was fortunate in that he got me at forty plus years of age. I had taken all the lessons that I perceived as failures (particularly the previous marriage) and applied those lessons to this new marriage. Being in this relationship is soo different. Yes, I think I am a different person, but I also learned a lot more through experiences. Some of those experiences were great and some of them were not. I learned things about myself that I am glad I outgrew and now I know better so I do better.

I no longer look at the first marriage as an example of me failing at something. I look at it for the gift it was at that moment in time and see the opportunity for growth that it eventually yielded to me.

I have set goals and failed to achieve them. But in hindsight, I realize that I achieved way more than I failed. When I have failed, I have picked myself up and kept going. Leaders have to be willing to take chances. We have to be willing to have contingency plans and the will to keep pushing because what I know for sure is that nothing worth having comes with ease. It requires hard work, focus, dedication and the ability to bounce. As in bounce back from rejection, unmet goals, loss and failures. I imagine without these experiences, we wouldn't really be able to savor the accomplishments when they happen!

Find the lessons that are to be had when you fail to achieve your desired goals. Spend more time in understanding the lesson so you can be ready to apply it the next time. Spending extra time in the disappointment and pain holds up moving forward. Focusing on the lesson prompts action — every single time.

Self-Reflection Challenge:
1. Does being accountable for decisions come easily to you? If so, why is that? If no, what fears do you have that are holding you back? How can you alleviate these fears?
2. Did you believe, before reading this chapter, that you were an accountable leader but changed your mind after the chapter? If yes, why?
3. How can you, as a leader, help others be accountable for their own leadership without micro-managing the situation or person?
4. Sometimes, leaders are good at being accountable for certain areas but struggle with others (e.g. employee management/disciplinary type issues). Are there specific areas of accountability that are easier or more difficult to you? Please explain.
5. Everyone fears failing at something. If you didn't you wouldn't be human! What are the three things you worry most about failing at? How do any of the things you listed prevent you from moving a goal forward?

6. Think back to a situation you would classify as a failure. What lessons did you learn that you later applied to another situation and were successful?

Chapter 12: Self-Care & Mental Health Wellness

In February of 2017 I was dizzy. Abruptly, suddenly, and with little warning, my life took an interesting wavy, curvy, disruptive course. I routinely drive the same route to work, like most of you. My commute is about thirty minutes one way, and I can do it with my eyes closed (please do not try that at home folks). On this particular day, when I pulled up to my parking space at work, I stumbled out of the car (there was no alcohol involved, I swear). It was weird and scary because I actually stumbled and I do not use that word for dramatic effect. It didn't stop me in my tracks, but it gave me significant pause. I pushed through it, made my way from the parking garage, up a flight of stairs, to an elevator, up twenty-three floors, then to my office. You know that feeling you get when you first step off a merry-go-round? Yeah, so that feeling was with me the entire time that I made the short journey from my car to the office. I began to panic, as in a panic attack. My heart was racing, I experienced hot flashes, and my anxiety was through the roof. I called my doctor to see if I could come in. Something wasn't right.

The visit to my doctor led to a series of three doctor visits within a three or four week time span. This path included my primary doctor, an ENT (ear, nose, throat) doctor and finally a neurologist.
The culprit that caused the above dizziness, inability to drive a car more than one mile, inability to work, panic attacks, and the countless subsequent episodes was severe vertigo caused by a vestibular disorder.

For time's sake, I won't be able to take you on the full journey of what the experience of having this level of vertigo was like because it lasted for months and is still with me today. What I want to do instead is show you how an unexpected disruption to your daily life functioning can impact your mental health.

Once I accepted what was happening to me was an actual "thing," I went to physical therapy for about two months to get better. Yes, there is physical therapy for vestibular deficits. Who knew? And it actually worked. Aside from the physical effects of the impact this level of vertigo was having on me, there was also a profound mental health impact. I felt frustrated that this was happening, and I didn't quite understand why. The cause was illusive and at the time, I was obsessed with trying to understand the cause of why this was happening to me. I would spend most of the night hours researching on the Internet (Google tells you everything you need or don't need to know) trying to figure out why. I got all kinds of possibilities of causes and wrote down the ones that seemed to make the most sense to me . . . and of course, I proceeded to take that list to my neurologist to show him I figured out the probable causes. After a patient sigh, a slight eye roll, and a "bless your heart" type of a shoulder pat, he asked me to focus on sleep in lieu of researching something I would be unlikely to find the exact answer to. Well that was frustrating!

I felt anxious, which is also synonymous with scared. I was in a constant state of fear. I didn't want to move. Like literally, not move my body at all. I figured out that if I just sat still, I wouldn't experience an episode (that is how I began to refer to the experiences of vertigo). Brilliant! Just sit still. I had the solution. This fear paralyzed me. I went days without stepping outside of the house (no sitting on the deck, no walking to the mailbox, no going to the garage, no looking out a window that was not from my bedroom).

All of those activities required that I get out of the bed and walk . . . and remember walking was the cause (per me) and I would just avoid that. I would go from my bed, bathroom, bed, bathroom, kitchen (that was a stretch) and repeat. During these days, the street my house is on was paved and I had no idea it had happened. I was constantly anxious and on the verge of a panic attack at any minute all the time.

When I reflect back on this time period, I would say to people, "I am lightweight depressed." I would often laugh behind it to make it not sound soo bad. The truth was I was depressed. If I wasn't anxious, I was sad. If neither of those, I was asleep. The sadness was because I felt like my whole life had been stopped in its tracks and I could not do the things I loved . . . or even just the "normal" things. There was a long period from diagnosis to completion of physical therapy, so months went by when I was just trying to adapt and cope to the weirdness of being in a constant state of imbalance, motion sickness, dizziness, depression, high anxiety and just feeling weird. It was exhausting.

What was happening to me was internal. You could look at me, and I would seem normal (especially if I just sat still). It was an odd dichotomy that made me feel that verbalizing my feelings would make me seem weird or crazy. I felt crazy to me so surely, I would to others. I had a wonderful support system at home and at work, but I still felt isolated, crazy, depressed and was a constant ball of high anxiety. Google led me to what started to give me hope. One night I googled some key words (I have no idea what they were) but it led me to https://vestibular.org/finding-help-support. Hold the phone, there are others like me? Others that use the same words to describe their experiences that I do? I am not alone? I read, read and reread. The more I read, the more I could feel myself coming back to life. Finally.

I am a trained mental health professional. I am a licensed therapist. I have over twenty years of experience working in mental health and I understand what anxiety and depression are. In spite of this, in the midst of my own challenges, I was not immune to experiencing a change in my own mental health wellness. A significant shift. People often think about mental health as an illness only. I would challenge us to think about mental health as a part of the continuum of health in the way we think about physical health.

A part of why there is such stigma associated with mental health is the shame we attach to it. Look back to my honest reflection of how I was feeling above. I was "afraid" people would think I was crazy. That is stigma.

Every single person reading this will or has experienced something that has impacted their mental health functioning. If we begin to talk more openly about changes to your health status because of your mental health, it will change the perception. Instead, we tend to talk about the most intensive, severe, dramatically portrayed on tv versions of mental health. I say to you — it is in all of our best interests to start understanding and being more mindful of taking care of our mental health just as much as our physical health. It may not be you today, but eventually you will be faced with managing your mental health wellness. Start today by being more cognizant of your own wellness and supportive of others suffering a decline or shift in their mental health. Everyday life factors impact your mental health wellness. Take the time to take care of yours so when life throws you a curve ball; you are ready for it all. Physically and Mentally.
##

The above was a blog entry titled, "Dizzy Depression" that I wrote to share my own experiences with mental health wellness. I hoped to spread awareness and shift the conversation to helping individuals understand that mental health impacts everyone, not just some of us. At any day, any moment, a shift can happen that impacts the health of our mental well-being.

However, what this story also points out is a common fallacy among women leaders in particular. We think we can do it ALL! We CAN but sometimes at a price if we do **not** take time for self-care. We tend to focus on what everyone else needs because one, we are built that way, and two it is what is expected. We have trained the people around us in our personal and professional lives to expect this and when we don't deliver, we feel some type of way.

I have shared a few personal stories with you so you might feel like you are getting to know me a bit! Well if that is true, the one thing you should know by now is that I think I am Superwoman. I really believe there isn't anything I can't do. That is of course, until I have passed the overload meter and keep trying to move forward! I think I am badass and it isn't until I often don't have a choice that I remember, *Ohhhhh, I am NOT really invincible. I really **do** need self-care and I do need to take care of myself as a priority and not after thought. Got it . . .*

The vertigo issue is still with me to this day, just not as severe as when it hit me in 2017. It is a part of who I am now and something I have to manage. The number one thing that reminds me that I still have this going on in my vestibular system is stress, and guess what? That's not the only body part that was trying to let me know I was going into overdrive.

Last year at my annual health physical, I had an unusual EKG reading and my (super BADASS Woman) doctor sent me immediately to a cardiologist. In the moment, I thought, *aren't we overreacting a bit*? I didn't have any notable chest pains, but when she asked me to think back over the past few months, I could recall having chest pains that I chalked up to indigestion.

With that information in hand, she had an appointment set up with a cardiologist within an hour (for the same day). She is aware of my busy life and responsibilities and insisted we take no chances. She ~~lectured~~ discussed with me the importance of not ignoring what may seem like simple symptoms when it comes to your heart (and really whatever) and gave me some devastating statistics of heart disease and women, particularly black women. YIKES. I was now not only annoyed that **one** appointment was turning into two appointments within the same day, but was also now scared to death that something was wrong with my heart!
Fast forward to later in the day. I make it to the cardiologist – yes! Another WOMAN doctor that was playing zero games with these subtle symptoms. I took a second EKG and it also read as "irregular." This was totally not the day I had in mind when I woke up. I started calculating the meetings I would need to move around and how this would really impact my schedule for the week. I know, don't argue with me . . . I was focused on the wrong thing. Lowers head in shame . . .

Within a week, I had an echocardiogram done and after impatiently waiting on the results, I learned that everything looked FINE. I underwent a stress test as a precautionary measure and I did fine with that as well. In the end, I was ok . . . except my blood pressure seemed to be a bit erratic. A slight adjustment to my medication and a conscious effort to maintain good eating habits seemed to level things out. Truth was, I had been stressed for quite some time.

This is what happens when you approach burnout. I would have never articulated that I felt any differently than normal because THIS WAS MY NORMAL. I was soo used to always being on "ten" that the high-energy, always moving, always thinking, always problem solving, always picking up new responsibilities, and always DOING something that <u>nothing less than that</u> felt normal. This incident with the heart scare was my body's way of getting my attention. The alarm bells were being rung, but this time it was a drill. I am not sure that the next time would have ended up like this story did if I hadn't heeded to the warning.

I did not write these chapters in order of importance, but if I had, this chapter would have been number one. You cannot be an effective leader for anything or anyone if you don't take care of yourself first. It seems obvious, but for whatever reasons you have, it is typically not how we operate. We will keep going until something forces us to do otherwise. I am working on this actively each day. I have not perfected this, but I am better at it than I was a year ago. Physical and mental health wellness are necessary components to being an effective, great leader but unfortunately, are the items we are likely to pay the *least* attention to until a crisis happens. Some of us excel at one or the other, but often not both. Some of you reading this may be able to check off all the boxes of self-care, but because demands on us and our forever evolving lives are always changing, self-care should evolve as well to keep up. A brisk walk used to perhaps work for you but now you need that plus something else just to feel peace. Whatever it looks like, we just need to make this a priority.

Another thing I see related to this is what I call the "self-martyr disease." This is the woman leader that overextends herself purposefully because she believes that this will prove or demonstrate her level of commitment. This is the individual in a leadership role that says yes to every request, comes in the office super early, leaves really late, and makes herself available to anyone who may need her around the clock. In a non-work setting this person looks the same. They say yes to every request a family member makes, yes to taking on a task that nobody else wants to do (e.g. host the holiday dinner at your house, plan the family gathering or reunion, take Aunt Whoever to her doctor appointments, find out why Cousin Such and Such said whatever she said about Cousin What's Her Name). Or, in a personal relationship, they are the giver and wonder why the other person is not giving back to them in the same way. Yet they continue to say yes to all the things they do not want to do and will stay in a relationship that doesn't seem equal.

While doing all of the above and more, they will complain about it. Yes, they also take a certain kind of pride in being the person who seems to solve everyone's problems, but they bring it to someone's attention as a complaint. It is actually not a complaint, as it is really intended to make sure you are aware of how awesome they are and how dedicated they are to tasks. These people burn out FAST. While they are burning the midnight oil to receive praise and genuinely help someone else, they are NOT taking care of themselves. How can they? If you aren't sleeping because you are constantly interrupted by phone calls for requests that require you to actually "do" something, you never get to reset from one day to the next.

There are many leaders who fall into this category. I would say many aren't aware of the toll they are taking regarding self-care nor do they know how to stop the above. It is hard to undo this when you have trained people in your life to treat you this way. Well, the solution to stopping the "self-martyr" syndrome is simple:

1. Recognize you are this person and want to be different.
2. Establish boundaries.
3. Learn to say no and be ok with it.

Self-care is multifaceted and requires different things for individuals as we are all unique and have varying degrees of needs. Making the decision to place this as a number one priority is the first step. Plan the trip, actually go on the trip, take the day off to just decompress, go on the date, jump on the trampoline at the indoor park with the kid, buy the shoes, get the spa treatment, light the candles around the bathtub, get the pedicure, have brunch, do WHATEVER it is that brings your soul comfort and your mind peace. Be the best version of you, so you can in turn be the best leader you can be. With that said, I am going to take a break and go eat! I am starving but didn't want to break my momentum!

Self-Reflection Challenge:

1. Have you experienced a medical (physical or mental) scare that let you know you may not be taking care of yourself?
2. Do you see the correlation between your leadership skills and your self-care strategies (or lack of)? How do you prioritize self-care in your life? If it is a high priority, what helped you get there? How can you help others that are still struggling with this around you?
3. Do you relate to the concept of the "self-martyr" disease? In what way? Is this you? If yes, what can you do about it?
4. What intentional thing can you do over the next twelve months that prioritizes your own health above everything else.
5. What is the correlation you see between your leadership style and the way you manage self-care?

Chapter 13: Integrity

Integrity for me means:
1. Doing the right thing even when no one is looking.
2. Being for the right thing even when it is not popular.
3. A willingness to stand on your belief system when faced with hard decisions.

Often people ask me about going into politics. I always respond with "that will never ever never ever never ever never ever happen." I have spent most of my career in public service and completely understand the sacrifices and hard work people in public service jobs experience. I also understand that for the most part, the jobs are thankless. I believe because so much of my background is in public sector, I had to figure out early on what integrity would look like **for me** and stand by it. Because if not, you could be the person on the news running from the investigative reporter! I don't want to be that person.

I have had the vantage point of watching many leaders come and go throughout my career of over twenty years. I observed what made some successful and others not so much. The most successful to me have been individuals who at the end of the day, had integrity. I am not defining success here as financial or being in a high-level position. Success to me looks like someone who came in, effectively understood the mission, was able to strategize and implement a plan (or several plans) to make significant changes that made a positive difference and leave with their reputation intact.

I always ask myself, *Is the work I am doing going to make a difference in someone's life?* If the answer is at least one person, I am moving forward. If the answer is that not one single soul will be impacted, it is not worth doing. I am motivated by doing things that yield noteworthy results. Having an impact on people's lives is a driver for me. However, I equally care about how I go about achieving goals. I want things to be **fair**. When I feel there is a sense of unfairness or inequality, I am the most irate. This is my Achilles' heel. If I don't feel like something is fair, it strikes at the heart of integrity for me. I use this in my leadership all the time unconsciously!

My mantra is, if it is at least fair, people will understand my "why." It's not about pleasing other people. I will never make everyone happy and neither will you. Fortunately, that's never my goal. My goal is to do the best I can and stay connected to my core value of integrity.

The actual definition of integrity is *"the quality of being honest and having strong moral principles; moral uprightness."* Integrity is one of those characteristics that takes on a specific meaning that may differ from person-to-person. See how the definition above can mean very different things per individual?

The best leaders that I have seen in my life have a sense integrity that is centered around something that is rooted in their impact on others. They are honest with those around them, provide transparent feedback, do not manipulate and genuinely work hard to achieve the common goals. Leaders who lack a clear moral center are more inwardly focused (self-centered) and are more likely to put themselves first while everything else falls in some order after that. Think about it, if you are on my team, essentially, I am your "boss."

Either I will manage you or lead you. There is a significant difference. If I lead you, I need to have a sense of purpose that extends to being interested in your success in addition to my own. If I am only interested in my own success, I will manage you but not lead you. This is not a bad thing; it is a reality thing. I may not be honest with you because I don't care about your growth; I only care about mine. I may give you feedback that you might perceive as critical because I am not interested in *you* learning from your mistakes and becoming better. I am only interested in managing you to get the work done. Whew, I felt like that one may have hit some of you too hard. Is it time for wine, coffee or tea again?

Since my core value is very much centered around fairness, it comes across in everything I do. I am completely fine with making a difficult decision as long as I believe it is a fair decision. I am completely fine with having to give critical feedback to a team member or peer because I want them to know exactly where I stand so they never feel blindsided. Why? Because that would not seem fair. I am okay with delivering a difficult message to a large group of individuals as long as it feels fair. The moment I am challenged and have to do something that does not seem fair, I struggle.

Now let me be clear, I know I cannot control external factors and the world around me. Life is not fair and that's the way things work. However, when it relates to how I approach leadership and integrity, I have core values that I hold on to as a baseline of how I start, period. It is also the "thing" that sparks leadership out of me in unplanned moments! Let me tell you about a time when my integrity forced me to lead outside of my box!

In 2018, I did something I never would have guessed in a million years that I would do. I joined a political ballot committee to stop a local cityhood referendum in my community. In short, the issue was that a few community members and former city officials, that lived in a cluster of gated country club communities, worked with legislatures outside of our represented area to do something that was quite unheard of.

The group formed a non-profit and started a process to form a new city by using unincorporated property from the county we live in. That in itself was normal and followed precedent of how previous cities had been formed across the state. What made it unusual was that in addition to forming the proposed new city via the unincorporated land, the group wanted to take thirty-three percent of the population and fifty percent of the business land from the existing city that neighbored many sections of the unincorporated parts of the county. It had never been done in the state's history and even nationally there were only a few scenarios that could be pointed to where anything close to this had been attempted. It was an attempted coup of an existing city in order to form a new city.

A legislative bill was written, shockingly passed, and ultimately signed by the governor at the time. The bill did not automatically allow for the new city to be formed, but it allowed for a vote by the citizens to determine if the city should be formed by stripping an existing city of a great portion of its population and major businesses. On the surface, that may still have not been so detrimental, but the vote had a catch. The only people who would be able to vote, would be the people who lived in the unincorporated area OR people that were mapped from the existing city to be moved to the proposed new city. The remaining individuals in the existing city would have **no vote** about the future of their city. I was a part of the "cannot have a vote" group. ***Wait what***?

To make this convoluted mess simpler, the existing city's population was about 29,000 and the number that would be eligible to vote out of that group was around 9,000. Huh? I had only been living in the community for about four years when this happened and began to think, *I should have gone with another city when I moved!* This was unbelievable to me. The news stations began to pick up the story and it became national news. I started to read everything I could about what was happening and started to attend local meetings by the city government (who were adamantly opposed to what was happening and several lawsuits were subsequently filed by the city). That's the background of the underlying issue. Can you see something that may have not set well with me and my sense of "fairness"? (Insert super hard side-eye here.)

While I am a registered voter, have consistently voted most of my adult life and consider myself to be a follower of politics, I never would have characterized myself as a political person per se (see the start of this chapter for reference on political aspirations). People often feel disconnected from politics and display a certain apathy towards voting and anything related to the political process. I get that. It is often hard to see the correlation between our daily lives and the people who are elected to run our cities, states, and federal government or the laws they pass. It is difficult to understand what it means to be a constituent to someone (rather you realize it or not) that is representing you and making decisions about your everyday life from afar until that decision impacts you personally. I was no different at the time.

I was not an active participant in democracy. I was a passive participant. I did my duty sometimes happily/excitedly and sometimes because it is what I was "supposed to do." I have likely voted for a referendum without fully understanding what the full impact would be (it sounded good enough, so I hit yes!) — but I still did not fully grasp how critical being truly involved is. As a now forever friend of mine has recently reminded me, democracy is NOT a spectator sport. But I admit, I was more of a spectator. Voting and not running from jury duty is not enough to make democracy work. So, out of anger, frustration and complete astonishment over this particular cityhood referendum, I stepped outside of my comfort zone and became an active, engaged citizen that was basically raging against the machine because I felt compelled to. How I see integrity was being challenged, and there was no way I would sit on the sideline.

I didn't believe the elected officials could just "handle it on their own" nor did I trust the process. I didn't trust the laws, which seemed to have loop holes everywhere, nor did I trust the "right thing" would prevail in the end without action. I didn't take this on alone, this required teaming with strangers. All people that I had no prior relationships with to fight for a common cause.

Listen, that part alone was MORE frustrating than the actual referendum issue. It was sometimes like an episode of *Survivor*. We lost some soldiers along the way and picked up new ones. I quit the committee in my head at least twenty-four times and one time for real for about two days.

My husband often complained about the amount of time it was taking away from our family but encouraged me to hang in there every time I threatened to quit.

I ~~argued~~ debated with all types of individuals on both sides of this referendum on social media platforms 24/7. We faced hurdles, disappointments, and challenges that would have made many decide it wasn't worth it. But that's the thing, it was absolutely worth it. If not us, then who would fight for our rights? It was not fair and I could not sit down even if I tried.

Yes, **we won** in the end as the voters responded at the polls with a resounding NO to this cityhood referendum and it was defeated. I am one thousand percent positive that if not for the commitment and leadership of our ballot committee, we would not have gotten the same results. Not a chance.

However disappointing it would have been to have lost, it would have not changed the experience. We pushed through knowing that we may or may not win because we HAD to. I personally persevered and experienced something that has forever changed me, and I will now be forever connected to this group of resistance fighters!

Yes, this was an experience for the books (no pun intended) and a pivotal moment for me personally. I am a better person and a better leader all because I got mad (really, really, really, mad) about something not seeming FAIR.

Great leaders understand that you have to stand for something and, in the process, remain TRUE to who you are. This is what integrity means to me. It likely means something different for you and that is okay. The biggest point is to know what your core value is that is nonnegotiable. If this is your anchor, stay anchored to it and hold steady. In the end, you will be rewarded because you satisfied your own soul.

Self-Reflection Challenge:

1. As discussed, integrity is a broad term. What does it mean for you? What is (or are) your nonnegotiable core value(s) that guide you?
2. For what you listed in number one above, how do the values (or value) shape you as a leader?

3. Some leaders lose their way over time. How can you stay in tune with your core moral compass as a leader and not float adrift?
4. Why do you think some leaders lose sight of integrity and seem to go with the wind as it relates to having a moral compass?

Chapter 14: Be Bold

Is there a certain type of personality that is required to be an effective, dynamic woman leader? Do you have to be an extrovert? Can introverts lead?

There is no one personality type that is required to be a great leader. Not all extroverts look the same and ditto for introverts. There are shared characteristics that I have found in dynamic leaders, but those same traits look differently on individuals. We all bring our own experiences, genetic makeup, and personality into how we lead. I hope by now you have caught on to a key point of this book. There is no one, perfect construct of a leader, but there are some traits that are required to be effective in the long term. For my introvert leaders, don't be taken aback by this chapter. **Being bold** is another lesson that I learned, over time, is required to be a good, effective leader.

This does not equal being reckless, but it does require coloring outside of the lines. The world is changing at warp speed around us. If you do what you always, did you will get what you have always gotten. You want something new and different; you must be willing to take a chance, put yourself out there, and go for it. How do you keep up with such a fast-paced, short attention span world and lead effectively? By being bold. Leaders look for the path to the solution when there doesn't look like one exists. Being bold allows you to be brave enough to say, "Why is it done this way?" And follow-up with a new idea when the response is "because that's the way we have always done things around here."

The opposite of bold is timid and unadventurous. How far will others follow you, listen to your guidance, and work towards collective goals if you are leading in a timid or unadventurous fashion? "Not many people" is the answer. People need to feel inspired by you. Feel encouraged by you. Feel empowered because of you. In order to elicit these feelings, it takes a little bit of gusto!

How do you stay in this lane over time? Easy, look for and be willing to do things that take you outside of your comfort zone. Take the adventure and do what is beyond your wildest dreams. Be ready for the opportunity that comes along, wakes you up from the mundane and reminds you there is a big world out there with lots to conquer. These opportunities help you lead better. The reason is, you learn that possibilities are limitless and you become more of a creative thinker. You are more willing to take a chance and bet on your "instincts." (Look at chapter one creeping back into the dialogue!)

The fact that I am writing this book is my "exhibit A "on the power of being bold. While I may think I have useful information to share that I really hope helps someone be the type of leader they want, writing an entire book about it is still pretty bold! However, there was a BOLD thing that happened to me that sparked this almost one year ago to the date.

It was a Friday afternoon and I had taken the day off work for a mental health day. Refer back to the self-care and mental health wellness chapter. I practice what I preach for the most part. Anyway, I remember exactly what I was doing when I received a text message from my boss. The message was brief and simply stated there was a possible opportunity to be interviewed on television with a major international news television network about suicide prevention. (This was around the time of the suicides of two well-known celebrities.) I took the message to mean I would need to prep my boss for the interview. Anticipating such, I reached out to members of my team to gather some recent statistics. Because of the recent deaths, the topic of suicide was in most major national newspapers and there was no shortage of perspectives on the issue. I began to read through those and felt pretty prepared to prepare my boss for what I assumed would be her interview.

About fifteen minutes had passed and I received a call from her. I answered, prepared to run down the most pertinent stats that I thought might come up for such an interview. As I began to let her know what I had done, she began to speak and somewhere in there, I heard "you" . . . "tomorrow" . . . "live." Hold the phone, literally! She kept talking and I quickly put the words together. My boss was telling me that I was going to do the interview, it would be live, and it would be in the morning at 6:30am. It was about 2pm when I looked at the time. I was stuck between astonishment, fear, anxiety, and did I say shock?

Okay, there are two things that I consider my sweet spot professionally and am willing to talk to anyone that will listen about:
1) Mental Health
2) Leadership

This was an opportunity to discuss mental health and anyone in the world could possibly see it. I was honored, ecstatic, and PETRIFIED all equally. By the time what was happening soaked into my thick skull, I was going through security live on the set the following morning at 6:30am. My husband rode with me and sat in the studio with me the entire time. He was the only person who knew how afraid I actually was. I had done radio and newspaper interviews before but never a live tv spot. Add to this the fact that I was speaking about such an important and sensitive topic. I wanted to get it right. I would have no opportunity for a do over. If I misspoke, I could impact someone's life. This had to be spot on.

There was no "dry run" or practice. One minute I was sitting in the studio watching a segment on finance and the next I was in a chair listening to someone countdown leading to "and go." I heard myself be introduced as an expert and I thought, *Hmmm I wonder who else they have for this segment*? Me, it was ME.

The interview was all of sixty seconds. It was a blur and just like that it was over.

It took me about four days to actually watch the entire segment. It was weird to see myself and I just wanted to say the right stuff. Watching it, I felt a like I did no harm, that I was more poised than what I imagined in my head and that was the most amazing experience, ever. I was full of gratitude for the opportunity and hoped that I helped at least one viewer.

Something else happened that day as well. This bold experience pushed me to feel like I should and could do more. I needed to color outside the lines, take chances and not be afraid to do things I have wanted to do. Speak more and write more. I was inspired and I have not looked back since.

These moments of opportunity present themselves and you have to be ready to take the step forward. Be bold enough to embrace the opportunity and the lessons that come along with it. This experience made me a better leader and person. It brought me to you.

We all need these moments of boldness to bring out pieces of ourselves that push us towards a more expansive path. We need them repeatedly so we can keep pushing ourselves. This is what begins to transform you into a dynamic leader. Are you willing to be as bold, creative and all the other things you expect from others you lead? Do they have examples of you demonstrating the type of leadership you want to see in them? This is what this is all about.

Be bold so that you can be inspiring to others. This is the stuff leaders are made of.

Self-Reflection Challenge:
1. Are you a transformative, bold leader? If yes, what are examples of this? If no, what is preventing you from being bold?
2. Can you see the correlation between being bold and the type of leader you become?
3. Was there an opportunity that would have allowed you to be bold that you passed up due to fear? If yes, what was the opportunity? What would you perhaps do differently?

4. Do you struggle with the concept of being bold and an introvert? If yes, remember this is not about personality type as much as it is about being willing to take chances. With that in mind, as an introvert, what does bold look like on you?

Chapter 15: Humility & Tolerance

The world is a hot mess right now. There is a lot wrong with how we are communicating with one another. I took a break from writing just for a couple of hours today, and it's like going from a library of welcome silence to being dropped off in the middle of the Atlanta airport.

A current event happening while I am working on this chapter is the number of states passing anti-abortion laws. I will avoid getting political here (again) and simply say, I hate that women's bodies are being politicized and their rights to their own reproductive health are being attacked.

I should be able to have my opinion and that be okay; just as I should be able to listen to your opinion and be okay with the fact that we might have different opinions. But I just spent about ten minutes of my life, that I cannot get back, reading people verbally attack one another on a social media site about this topic. Complete strangers calling each other names such as but not limited to "idiot," "liar," "murderer," "racist," "dummy," "asshole," and so forth. It is exasperating. Well guess what? Many of these people are a part of the workforce and, wait for it, some of them are leaders. They are leading other people, businesses, churches, Girl Scout troops, PTA, cities, counties, states, countries, ETC. This is what we have been reduced to. So, if name calling and being unwilling to hear from people that may be different from you, without arguing, is ramped up on social media, how are we communicating in real life?

In a professional setting this may look like the person who hires people who are exact replicas of their own personality. By doing this, you end up building a team of people who all will think like you or approach problem solving in the same way as you. It also increases the likelihood that you will have less tolerance for opposing views or opinions. This is lazy! Understanding how to build a team of independent, critical, outside the box thinkers is the sign of good leadership. Being willing to tolerate differences of opinions respectfully and being open to another person's approach are the signs of a great leader. There is a difference between the two types of leaders. Test this out if you are having difficulty digesting this concept. Look at any high functioning leader that you may know. Then look at the team they have built around them. Do they all mirror the personality traits of the leader? Do they all have similar shared experiences? How diverse is the team culturally? All of the answers to the questions posed will tell you everything you need to know about how tolerant that leader is.

This tidbit is such a critical part to being not just great but dynamic in your leadership role, so put down the wine glass because I really want this point to stick. If you can master the art of being able to sit with a group of diverse individuals, process all the various points of view, take in the perspectives and motivations of each person and allow yourself to be informed by all information (as opposed to the approach you already had neatly laid out in your head), then you will be dynamic in your leadership approach. It is really this simple, yet complicated, because we are flawed individuals. We want things the way we want them and, of course, we know what's right because why else would we be here? Ha! Nope. Not true at all. We are always growing in our leadership and having the tolerance to be open to learning more, being more informed, and incorporating other perspectives is the true key to mastering this skill.

Great, now you have either realized you are already tolerant and have this part down to a science or you just had an ah-ha moment and need some time to reflect. If the latter is true, pick the wine glass back up because it just gets bumpier from here ladies!

The second lesson I've learned over time, that is a close cousin to tolerance, is **humility**. Here's the thing about humility: you can never lose it. This is not negotiable. Leaders that lack the ability to express humility, or to be humble, will crash and burn eventually. Their flaming star they exuded, that took them to the top of their career, will expire without humility.

An excellent leader will do the following as necessary:

1. Admit they were wrong.
2. Apologize and mean it with action.
3. Look for ways to make other people be successful.
4. Remain grateful for anyone who helped them over time.
5. Recognize that they alone cannot solve all the problems and need to be able to work with other people for better results.
6. Always respect people regardless of their positioning, title, or role. You may be on top today and back at the bottom tomorrow.

You cannot do any of the above if you lack humility. This isn't identified in just the things you say to people; it is reflected in your total aura. People know humility when they see and feel it. I think women are often better at this than men mostly because we are nurturers by nature. However, even with that advantage, I have seen women be some of the worst offenders of this. Usually it's because they don't have someone around them to help identify their blind spots and show them when they fail at this. Remember, if everyone around you is just like you, who is going to even notice it? I'll tell you who . . . everyone else that you interface with that says, "There's just something about her I don't like," or "Something about her feels arrogant or snobbish." These are sometimes code words that you should not be dismissive of. Perception matters. What you do about humility and tolerance, as a part of your character, says more about you often than anything else. Being cognizant of your levels of tolerance and humility are essential for any great leader.

I started out this chapter talking about mean people. Let's end it with a blog entry I wrote previously about how to be kind! Nice way to close this chapter out.

Be Kind, Do Good

Counties here in metro Atlanta, Georgia are reporting a record high advanced voting turnout. These trends seem to also have a national correlation as well; meaning, several states are reporting this same information.

Happening simultaneously is a series of bombs that have been sent to Democratic Party leaders or outspoken advocates. In the midst of all of this and a large amount of other reasons, the political climate of the country is one of division and we are experiencing a unifying leadership gap. This observation isn't about political party affiliation and party control. It is about something much bigger than that. What is happening now is a search for the moral compass that should guide our country. It is MIA.

Social media has done wonders for bringing people together. Sort of like how I am talking to you right now from the comfort of my home with my feet kicked up and a glass of wine to my right. However, what has also happened is that people have access to information at warp speed — accurate or false — but still information. This fast pace and open access to humans across the globe also creates a sense of perceived power that emboldens a lot of us to say and do things we would never say and do in real life to one another. It is out of control and extremely overwhelming for most.

Do not fret! All is not quite lost. There is something you can do even when it seems like the opposite is true. Of course, exercise your right to vote if you choose, but that is one step. The other, and for me, very critical for managing your own mental health wellness is to counter the negative draining energy by this . . . wait for it . . . Be kind and do good.

Before you boo me off the stage, hear me out. I often leave the Internet feeling defeated by all the tribalism, mean girls on steroids (except it is more like "mean people"), that I'm soo energized about voting or posting a comment (or several) that my good vibes are sucked out of me or I am simply exhausted. So, what I do is leave the house and interact with real humans and look for opportunities to be kind and do good.

1. I spend a little extra time in my local grocery store and ask the employees in the deli how has their day been. I say "thank you" and "yes ma'am" and wish them a great rest of their shift. AND if they cut my deli turkey exactly the way I want (not to thin, not to thick), I tell them they are the best humans walking the earth. And I mean every word of it!

2. No matter how much I am rushing to a meeting, when on the elevator, I say "hello" when I don't feel like it, but I always feel a bit better after I do. If I see someone is rushing to catch the elevator, I risk my right arm to halt the doors from closing. I enjoy the look of gratitude and relief when that person realizes they WILL make the elevator.

3. When I see a senior citizen struggle with anything, I ask if I can help. If they insist, they are good, I am still pleased that I offered and in awe of their bad-azz-ness.

4. When driving, if I am in the slow lane and someone is merging, I make it a point to slow down and assist them in the merging process. On this same note, if someone lets me over in traffic, I always blow my horn and wave at them from the window. I want them to see I am thankful. (Disclosure: I also use the same car horn when I am unhappy about how someone else is not "nice" out here in these Atlanta streets. I'm just saying…

5. When someone is in line in front of me at Kroger (grocery store) and they don't have a Kroger Plus Card, I gladly offer up mine. (Disclaimer: It makes me equally as happy because I am going to get some more points . . . but still . . . don't get stuck there).

Those are five things I do frequently in order to be kinder and do good in my neighborhood. Find your five things you can do each day. No, it will not change the tenor or the atmosphere OR the division in our country right now, but it WILL make you feel a little better — a little bit at a time. It will help you/us connect to humans and remember, for a moment, that underneath it all (and in spite of the rhetoric and shit talking from keyboard bullies), we are more alike than we are different. It will remind you that humans thrive when there is a feeling of connectedness. It will be good for your mental health WELLness. And you might change someone's perceptions or perspective one kind act at a time.

Self-Reflection Challenge:

1. Think of the last time you were wrong about a decision you made or an action you took. How did you handle being wrong? In hindsight, is there something you wish you had done differently?
2. Not all leaders are humble or tolerant of differences. In spite of that, I am here telling you to NOT be that leader. Do you believe that those types of leaders are actually more successful? If yes why? If no (which I hope you pick!) why is that in your opinion?
3. What are things you can do to practice humility and tolerance every day in your own life?

Chapter 16: The Trio: Intelligence, Curiosity, Methodical

Facts still matter and being a nerd is IN. It is an absolute "cool kids club" to embrace being smart.

No matter what you may be told when you turn on your television or read a news piece on the Internet, I promise you that if you are a critical thinker and have a level of intellect that is above average, you are still winning. It seems as though it would be a given to say that any effective leader has what I call the trio: intelligence, curiosity and a methodical way of approaching more complex issues. However, it is not a given and, in many instances, some are shamed for being "smart."

Girlfriends listen, successful leaders do need to be smart. I don't just mean educated. They are not one in the same. You can have various educational degrees and not be smart. Let's not conflate the two here. Smart, intelligent people gather their information, over time, in all types of ways. It may be from an education that was received from schools or the streets or real-life experiences that shaped your thinking over time. Avid readers become more informed not just because they absorb a variety of information, but they expand their vocabulary and knowledge base while turning on the creative side of your brain. Intelligence is acquired over time and is ever evolving. Actively engaging in things that keep you learning versus those that keep you stagnant or from wanting to learn more, is a choice you make every day.

I did it today! I woke up and I had a choice. Do I reach for my phone and see what is happening on social media? Or, do I find something to actually stimulate my brain into a learning mode. Today, I chose the latter. Yesterday I chose the first. Ha! The point is, I actively choose things to push my thinking but it's not overkill. I don't expect you to go overboard either. I simply want you to not lose sight of this: No matter how you got the leadership role you are in, to maintain the position and continue to excel, you have to feed your brain with knowledge.

Think about the people you spend most of your time conversing with in a week. Check your circle because it is these people that influence you the most. What are they teaching you? Does it add value to your life, make you smarter, or keep you stagnant?

Do these individuals help you learn or do they keep you in the same space? Do these individuals teach you new ways to look at a situation? Or, do they cosign whatever you say? Do these individuals teach you something completely new that helps you approach a specific topic in a new way? Do you learn at least one new thing a week?

Depending on how you answered, those questions will let you know some changes you may need to make or opportunities for improvement. Embrace learning as a lifelong venture. It adds value to your intellect. Don't let the simple, basic distractions of life take you too far away from maintaining your quest for knowledge. Practically speaking, in a professional environment, you have to be willing to ask questions when you are confused. Some people prefer to play along as though they understand what is happening even when they do not. Others (ME) will stop an entire conversation/meeting when they are not following what is happening.

I like to be certain and I seek out additional information when I am confused. I can't move forward in a state of confusion or uncertainty; that's just who I am. My dad always jokes that I short circuit when things don't make sense. It is not a joke; it is the truth! For me, I need to seek out the information that is not as transparent. I need to ask questions to make sure I am clear about the strategy. I feel a strong desire to understand the "why" about any move so I can navigate my way to the end result. I am not embarrassed when I don't understand a conversation, a plan, or strategy. I believe that if I am confused there is a high likelihood that someone else in the group is feeling the same way. We have been told for most of our lives that "no question is a stupid question." I believe this to be true when you have an honest goal of seeking to understand to improve your knowledge base and inform your decision making.

A very smart leader that I admire, always says, "be curious about what you don't know." I live by this! Seeking out clarity, alternative perspectives, new information, exploring why something is the way it is, being open to finding new approaches and more all fold into this one sentiment. When there is a strategy that is not working, be curious about why that might be. You have a relationship that is not the way you had hoped it would be; have curiosity to seek out understanding. Is it you or them? The way we communicate on social media is telling of how we are starting to communicate in real life. We talk at each other versus to each other. We don't engage in debate seeking to understand both sides; we seek to only hear our one side and close our ears, eyes, and minds to anything that appears to be different. It is the way much of the current leadership is working in our country, so it is no wonder society started to become molded this way.

I say to you, if you are going to be an effective leader, you learn from what is happening with leadership in our country right now. Try to understand why it is happening; be curious about different perspectives and use that information to inform you. It will help you decide what kind of leader you want to be.

Last, I mention in the trio — methodical. This for some is more of a character trait than a lesson on leadership, but I think it is both. Being methodical, to me, means the ability to have foresight and plan accordingly. Of course, best made plans . . . often do not go as planned, but do not be deterred! People have asked me why I think I am an effective leader. One of the traits that I often cite is that I am methodical. I am a "doer person" — likes to see something happen and not spend a lot of time processing it. However, I care about the how things get done. I touched on this earlier as far as communication and assertive conversations. Here, I mean it a bit differently. Being intelligent, curious, and methodical go together perfectly. As stand-alone items, they don't quite give you the full recipe you need for greatness as a leader.

- You can be smart but not effective as a leader.
- You can be curious about what you don't know and that make you nosey.

- You can be methodical but that can also keep you stagnant because you spend most of your time planning but never achieving.

The trio together is where the magic happens. Having the intellect to develop a strategy/goal; the methodical thinking to plan out what will be necessary to achieve the goal; and the curiosity to seek out information you will need to be successful and sustain the effort is the perfect combination of what it really means to be smart! This is the nerd in me living her best life right now. This is my sweet spot. You have to find the way to make this work for you. In doing so, here are some major takeaways for your consideration as a woman leader:

1. Being intelligent is not the degree(s) on your wall or the letters behind or in front of your name.
2. Being intelligent is the accumulation of your educational experiences, real-life application, environmental learnings and exposure, and social adaptability.
3. Intelligence is a lifelong experience and should peak only when you are no longer living. You are an evolving human being with the opportunity to learn something new daily to add to your arsenal of intellect.
4. Curiosity that children have (they ask the best questions) should not stop as an adult. Continue to question rules, policies and other things that just do not make sense to you. Seek out more information to be informed so that you can appropriately challenge systems.
5. Have a path for all that you do. Sure, on occasion you will just luck out. Without a plan or preparation, you get what you want. That will not be the case in the long haul and it is not sustainable. Have the ability to formulate a plan that is methodical.

If you can master this trio of being a nerd 101, you will become an effective leader. If you feel as though you have this already mastered and no additional work is required on your part, you have missed the point. Go back to number three above.

Self-Reflection Challenge:

1. The challenge of checking your inner circle and looking at how you seek out new information to help you learn, is not something we do naturally. Having asked you to consider this, what did you learn about who is shaping your learnings?
2. Can you commit to two things weekly that do not involve social media, but that help you nurture brain and intellect health?
3. What will you do differently as a result of thinking about the trio as you continue on your leadership journey?
4. As a leader, how can you help promote the concepts of the trio for those that you have influence over?
5. What is something that you wish you did more of to seek out new information (being curious about what you don't know)? What is preventing you from doing what you identified? Can you now develop a plan to put this in place?

Chapter 17: Conflict Management

It is no accident that I saved conflict for the end of the quarter or that it came after the *trio* chapter. This chapter alone is an all-day workshop and more! However, I will attempt the impossible and cover what you need to know <u>most </u>about managing conflict. Let's get some fundamentals out of the way first to set the stage:

1. A conflict can only exist if **two or more** are involved. A conflict with a party of one does not make a conflict.
2. Not all disagreements equal conflict.
3. Despite what you may believe, even when you have been legitimately wronged, the longer you engage in the conflict, the longer it will last.
4. There is always a role you play in the conflict whether you perceive that to be true or not.

Several years ago, I experienced something that I never had before. I was in an actual conflict with my direct supervisor. Someone insert Black Rob's "Whoa" song here — or go to YouTube and search for it so you can have the appropriate background music as I take you on this journey. For the most part, I am a fabulous, proud, ambitious nerd who always gets along with the supervisor. For reference, this has been true since the pre-k three progress report card I shared with you earlier. Ms. Heard's seventh grade classroom is another example of this.

Some teachers leave an everlasting impact on the lives they touch, and Ms. Heard was one of my earliest examples of what a fabulous, flawless effective leader looked like. I gravitated to her, and for me, that meant I sat as close to the front of the classroom as possible, I made sure to turn in all my assignments on time and I used interpersonal skills that I didn't know I had at the time to woo her. She was known as no-nonsense and she played the part well. The biggest take away from observing her was that she did it with grace, class, and a level of fabulousness that I took note of and has been forever engraved in my psyche. Even at this age, I knew she was something special and a very early indicator of the path I would take in the future. At the end of the school year, I won one of the most coveted superlatives — **teacher's pet.** Winning this award was special for me and *to* me. It meant that despite her no-nonsense approach to teaching, she said to me (without saying it directly), that I was special to her also.

From that day forward, I learned (purposefully or subconsciously) that is was best to get along with those that have a position of authority over you. This was modeled for me early on. Who knew I'd pull these traits out thirty-something years later?
For the sake of the conflict story, you know by now I don't use real names, (except for Ms. Heard because she deserves the shout-out!) we will call this particular supervisor I am referencing from earlier in my career, *Mitzi*.

Mitzi was an older white woman in the latter part of her professional career and I was a younger black woman that finally had a seat at the grown-up table with other leaders. I would say I was right in the middle of flourishing as a leader but with a lot more growing to do. This was a challenge I was up to and sought out, whenever I could, opportunities for growth. We both were ambitious and shared traits that I thought would complement one another in a duo. I do not think I have ever been as wrong as I was about any of what I just wrote before.

While all of these things initially seemed like positives for a good professional relationship, it ended up being quite the opposite. Initially, we got along well. This had always been my experience with a supervisor or manager as I had never "gotten into trouble" before in a work setting and was never chastised. Remember, I am a nerd and I tend to focus on having positive relationships and getting the goals achieved. I don't make enemies on purpose (although I know now, sometimes by virtue of being who you are, you can and will develop some along the way if you stick around long enough). I also learned in seventh grade that being the teacher's pet was much more rewarding in the end. Imagine my discomfort when I realized the original dynamics that I thought would be positive about my relationship with Mitzi did *not* turn out to be anything like what I thought.

As things notably shifted in our relationship, I figured out the dynamics I perceived between us along the way were way off base. The reality was she was more ambitious than I was at the time and I was in her way. Mitzi had plans to be more and do more and there was an odd dichotomy that had been set up with us. She co-managed me along with someone else. The other partner in this situation was someone I actually learned a lot from and still admire to this day. It was like having two parents in a work setting and it was weird. Nonetheless, the structure would have been manageable had there not been the obvious disconnect between Mitzi and I.

It appeared that she didn't quite know what to do with me. From my perspective, I wanted to do what I always do — my job and have the space to do so. Instead, I found that I was spending most of my time on the defense from subtle acts from Mitzi designed to undermine almost everything I did. Whoa. This was new territory for me. I spent many days, weeks, and months trying to understand why this was happening. It is in my nature to seek out understanding when I feel confused. I ultimately realized we were in a power struggle whether I wanted to be or not. Mitzi did not have anything that I wanted, but I apparently had things she wanted. I was seemingly in the way of her ambitious plan to gain/take more power and control. Unfortunately for us both, she thought that meant directly undermining me and challenging most of what I did. It was not because I was *not* doing my job or because I was doing something that warranted this approach. It was because I was who I was. In lieu of being seen as an asset, I was seen as a barrier. I went from being confused to being angry.

Our conflict started out as a series of small, petty actions targeted towards me that could easily be disguised as something other than what I knew it to be. A gentle stab here or there to remind me who really was in charge. This could be a charged email, veiled with just enough tone to take me aback. Or, it could be a glare that was meant to "put me back in my place." From there it moved to much more obvious actions such as intervening with my team members to spread the message that I could not be relied upon. If the staff really wanted their needs addressed, they were better off going to her and she would be sure to "handle it." It moved past passive aggressive behaviors to overt actions that had clear messages.
I became more adept at predicting her next move and learned several work arounds. I figured, after all, the hard work I had done would stand on its own merit. If she wanted to banish me, she didn't have the power to do diddly squat.

This revelation (the story I was telling myself) of course emboldened me like nobody's business. I set out on a path to resist her every move and make it clear to her that I was aware of what she was doing and would not be pushed out. While I felt like my feelings were one hundred percent justified, I was wrong. As the universe always has a way of doing, it sent me guidance. Remember the co-manager infrastructure I told you about earlier? Well, I had just about had it with Mitzi and was frustrated with my "other manager" for not helping me! Could he not see what she was doing? He was smart and had always been super supportive of me. Why was this a blind spot for him? I didn't know so I reached out to him for insight and guidance.

He acknowledged that he knew Mitzi and I were having a really hard time getting along and he wished it were not happening. Hell, me too! This conflict was causing me to be in a constant ball of knots. I wanted to call out of work if it would mean avoiding Mitzi as I was not sure of how long I could allow her to keep pushing me. By this time my agenda was **not** to work with her and I became consumed by focusing on how to expose her for what I perceived to be fallacies in her character and behavior.

After hearing me vent on the subject for what seemed like hours, he offered this advice: "Monica, I know you are angry. But to resolve the conflict, you have to also look in the mirror and determine how you are contributing to the conflict."

WHAT?!?!? I was appalled and didn't speak to him, unless I had to, for days. I was adamant there was no need to look in the mirror for anything because it would simply prove my point — I was not the problem; SHE was the problem. How could he not see what was happening? He agreed with my assessment of Mitzi but made no effort to fix this (in my head). Instead he continued his thought with, "I think you just need to talk to her." That was a negative and I had zero interest in being the bigger person. I felt aggrieved, agitated, disrespected and my morale was at an all-time low.

Days later, I processed his words and began to make a shift from my earlier thinking. His words of advice, that I brushed away initially, played like an endless loop in my head. It ended up being an everlasting statement about leadership: "<u>Look in the mirror and determine what role you are playing to keep the conflict going</u>." I struggled to apply his feedback to this situation. You see, in my mind, I was the victim. I was being bullied and I was pissed. I wondered how this conflict where I was the victim and she was the aggressor turn into "I need to look into *myself*?" Well, needless to say, I was positive that I WAS NOT THE PROBLEM. That is, until I had time to process the advice. Was I a part of the problem after all? Was there something I had done to make this conflict exist and grow legs? The answer was <u>yes</u>.

Yikes. It took me a while to do the true inner reflection and look at and *own — be accountable for —* how I responded to the mistreatment that I perceived was happening to me. I contend to this day that this individual woman was wrong and I was right. But that did not mean that I didn't play a role in keeping the conflict going. I was on a mission to disconnect our relationship in order to be further removed from the scenario. I was angry and I let my emotions make most of my decisions.

It was <u>fortunate</u> that we were forced to continue working together. Had we not, I would *not* have had the experience of learning the lesson that was hiding in the drama. Despite being Ms. Heard's "teacher's pet," I would not always be everyone's cup of tea. I couldn't change Mitzi, but I **could** change how I chose to respond to the issues. This was not an easy conclusion to come to because I felt like an aggrieved victim. All I could make sense of, in my head, was that she or I would need to leave in order for me to find peace. In the real world, you cannot banish people you do not like or disagree with. This is what I tried to do to no avail.

However, what did work was the introspection and thinking about how I was indeed playing an <u>active role</u> in the conflict. I began to change my outlook and attitude. I re-examined some of my behaviors that I chose:

- Did I sometimes make her wait longer for an email reply in a basic power struggle? Yes, I did.

- Did I purposefully avoid any individual time with her? You bethca.
- Did I begin to inadvertently lead my team in a way that made them feel like it was okay and acceptable to not like Mitzi either? Yes, I did.

I could see the snowball effect in how my behavior and actions (as right as I thought I was) were impacting the people around me and my own credibility as a leader. I realized in the end I was ***not*** being an effective leader at all. I was more interested in proving that Mitzi was wrong and needed to be held accountable for her actions towards me; there was nothing anyone could do or say to tell me otherwise at the time. What I failed to do was take earlier responsibility for my part in the conflict. I got there, but it took some time. I used to be upset that I utilized so much time on this conflict, but now know that it was necessary to get to the next level of leadership. Mitzi taught me several things throughout all of that mess:

1) I became more accountable for actions I choose to take.
2) I became more resilient.
3) I learned things about my character as I went through that period of adversity.
4) She made me a better leader in the end.

There are always opportunities to learn and grow in the midst of a struggle or conflict; we just have to be willing to take the lessons regardless of how they may be taught to you.

Mitzi and I never got to a place of full reconciliation. That was never the goal for either of us. We did, however, get to a place where we were able to exchange pleasantries. This was good enough because I got my sanity back and had peace. She eventually moved on and I eventually moved up and needed to have this experience in order to thrive. For that, I am thankful.

While this story is shared with you through my lens and my perspective, it is how I experienced the conflict. Mitzi's perspective may be different and that is absolutely okay. Conflict is not about agreeing on perspectives. It is about controlling the one thing you can control — you. Conflict only thrives when it is being watered or fed. I was absolutely playing a role in keeping the conflict alive in this story! I was too close to the scenario and couldn't see it in the beginning.

What I now know is that resolution to conflict is not about everyone walking away taking ownership of their role or even feeling apologetic. Sometimes you get the apology and sometimes you don't. Sometimes you give the apology and sometimes you don't. Instead, I know to always look inward for my role in the conflict and determine what I can do to stop the conflict from growing. Humility is about saying you are wrong when you are wrong. Resolving conflict is about looking at yourself to determine how you can manage the experience. Conflict isn't always bad. However, it is always an opportunity to learn something new and grow. Nobody can do this *for* you. Only you can take a hard look at YOU and determine which factors are being contributed by you. This is applicable in all aspects of life. Remember that attempting to control other people's behavior, choices, decisions or assumptions is fruitless and an exhausting exercise. Save that energy to help yourself be the leader you desire to be.

Self-Reflection Challenge:

1. Conflict brings us an opportunity to learn and grow. Think of a conflict experience you have gone through and the impact it had on you as a leader.
2. I know that I am stubborn. It is a trait I have that can interfere with conflict. What are your traits that can escalate a conflict? How will you plan to manage them?
3. Conflict resolution does not always end with a hug or an apology. If you do not get this as a leader, how will you manage it? Will you hold a grudge? Will you feel like you did not resolve the conflict?
4. Conflict is not bad all the time. Think of a conflict you have experienced that was not a bad experience but taught you an important lesson.

Chapter 18: Love & Support

He loves me, he loves me not.
Now why on earth would there be a chapter about love? Didn't I say
I *could* write about relationships earlier but would save that for
another time? I lied just a little bit. The role of love plays a pivotal
part in a leader being effective and great! It may not be obvious but
it does.

The overall construct of this book focuses on being an empowered,
effective woman leader. We have covered an assortment of critical
skills and lessons that I believe are critical to success. This chapter
focuses on the power of love and support. I get it — it doesn't seem
like a chapter about love would exist within this construct but, oh
yes, it absolutely does! Without a doubt, one of the lessons I have
learned about leadership is this: Love is key to effective leadership
and a generally happy life.

You will be knocked down quite a bit in your career or day to day
life in general. You will sometimes win and sometimes fail. You will
be on top at times and other times climbing back from the
knockdown. You will have conflicts related to work/career and will
want to just walk away but know that you must push through
regardless. You will simply have good and bad days. For all of this
and more, you need love around *and* in you.

Love is a safety net that automatically opens to help hold you
together when it seems that nothing else will. Love presents itself in
many ways and comes from a plethora of sources: romantic love,
family love, pet love, friendship love, spiritual/religious love, etc. are
all examples. Whatever the type, I know for sure that love aids you
in multiple ways along your career and life in general. Here are a
few examples:

1. Being loved the way your heart truly desires, romantically, takes time to find and for you to sort out what that means for you. Taking the time to kiss some frogs to find a prince or princess is worthwhile because once you have the right partner by your side, <u>everything</u> changes. You become more emboldened to try your dreams. You aren't afraid to try something new in your life because you have a good partner that loves you, motivates you, and picks you up if you fall. It allows you to push harder for your goals because you have a cheering section right next to you even when you don't realize you need the support. Being *in love* is not a constant, it changes over time and requires work and investment; however, being loved is soo much more powerful and is sustainable through good and bad times. Therefore, carefully choosing who you share your romantic love space with is powerful and worth being purposeful in your selection. When you have chosen wisely, you will know because it bleeds into all areas of your life, including your professional environment.

Love provides you with an extra layer of protection as you face the challenges that exist in your career or just the outside world in general. Knowing how you want to be loved and being willing to do the internal work, to be ready to receive the love your heart desires, are all things you control. Romantic love is tricky and unpredictable so taking the time to get this right not only is worthwhile for your own personal happiness, but it makes everything else around you that much easier to cope with because you have the partner that was intended for you. This person wants you to succeed and will sacrifice to ensure your dreams come true. You and this person want each other to succeed and will both sacrifice to ensure that both of your dreams come true. Take the time to make sure your number one fan deserves the spot. It is too important of a position to not get right.

2. Unromantic friendship love is critical. We need our girls (and guys)! We need good friends that know us and sometimes outlast any romantic love. These friends listen to whatever you need to vent about, are honest with you and tell you what you don't always want to hear (but need to hear). Being able to have a circle full of friends that have goals, dreams, and do whatever it takes to support one another, in a way only a good friend can do, is key. I read an article recently about the importance of girl trips and just time with friends. It is special when you have friends that feel like family because they KNOW you, support you even when you may not think you need it, (and of course when you ask for it) and love you despite yourself. With the right friends, you will feel empowered to take on anything. At least with the ones I have, that is true . . . if it's not for you, check your circle ASAP.

Eliminate dead weight and those that want to be your friend but don't know how to be a friend in return. It brings your energy down, plays with your emotions and takes time away from you focusing on achieving whatever goals you may have. Again, choose who you allow to have this type of access and influence in your life. Once this circle is filled with those that want to see you succeed, want to empower you and do not feel like it is a competition, you will feel supported and empowered to go after your dreams. In the end, if you need help cleaning your bruises from a battle, they will be there on the other side with open arms to motivate you to keep going.
 Everyone doesn't need access to you. Protect your friend circle space as you would with family. Having the right people and energy in this circle is important and we don't have time to give away your goal-oriented energy to people that aren't there to truly support you.

3. Family love is complex because families are complex. Families are also defined differently for some. I approach this one with simply this: family love is unconditional. For me, I am fortunate in that I have key family members that I love deeply and vice versa (My brothers, aunts, uncles, my cousin-sister, a ton of other cousins, bonus kids, bonus in-laws, etc.). I am blessed to have a dad that has cheered me on since my earliest memory of him. He instilled in me that I could and would be anything I wanted to be. I have a dad that reads and critiques everything I have been writing for the book because he wants me to be successful. I have a dad that listens to my work stories and gives me on the spot advice even if he isn't feeling his best at the time. I have a mom that is a silent supporter. She loves me and is proud but expresses it differently. It is okay that they are different because I know for sure they will always be there for me. I am lucky in that way. Everyone isn't born into a similar situation and that is OKAY because along the way you meet people that transform into family because family is not always about blood. Whatever family looks like for you, they matter and can serve as a support for you when others disappear.

5. Mom (or parent) love is special. Whether you are a mom to biological children, inherited, bonus (step-parent), god-mom, or whatever! The love you feel as a mom is like nothing else that can be explained. Children have a way of grounding you like nobody's business! They are honest critics and tell it like it is. Being a mom changes your entire perspective on life. The love mothers have for their children is a force that is hard to reckon with. That same force can drive women to dream big and want to achieve success because they want the best for their children. It is a powerful motivator like none other. You can use this love to help you master pretty much anything in the universe. Being a mom is the hardest job I have ever had by far. It isn't easy raising human beings. But moms do it along with a million other responsibilities. Imagine taking all those same skills and applying them to how you lead? It will yield a positive outcome. Having children can fill your heart with joy; when the world is tripping, you can look to your children to have unconditional love for you and vice versa. It's powerful.

6. Self-love is the hardest of the list. Yes, even harder than finding the perfect partner for yourself (see romantic love section above). Self-love is taught through a series of experiences. Some of those experiences teach you to hate or love yourself. You also teach people how to love you. If you don't love yourself, what are you teaching others about loving you? Self-esteem issues and self-love issues are synonymous to me. If you don't love you, then honestly, who else will? This isn't a new philosophy, but it needs to be reiterated here. When I look at successful and unsuccessful women leaders, this concept is a deal breaker for success.

For example, people that are insecure, filled with doubts about their abilities, self-sabotages and without love for themselves are horrible leaders. Their insecurities come across in how they lead. They belittle others and don't nurture growth in others because they are insecure about their own positioning. They strive for conflict to distract from their own inadequacies. I hate to be this blunt, but this one is so critical I cannot afford for the point to be missed. Learning to love yourself is not arrogance. It is self-preservation that leads to a healthy you and a more effective leader. Period. People that don't love themselves have difficulty loving others and forming good interpersonal relationships with other people. If you cannot form positive relationships with peers, colleagues, etc., then how can you be successful in the long run?

Self-love is the inner voice that tells you when to take a break and focus on yourself. It is the voice that tells you someone's energy is not going to be beneficial for you in any way and to have the courage to remove that person from your space. Self-love is walking away from a romantic love that is doing more harm to you than good, despite what your heart wants. Self-love is about accepting nothing less than what you believe you truly deserve. It is also about setting boundaries and being unapologetic about enforcing them to protect your space. Self-love is about being true to you, putting your needs front and center and not believing that you must put yourself last to make everyone else around you happy. On airplanes when they go over the safety procedures, they repeat the same phrase each time — *"Put your oxygen mask on first before trying to help others."* Same rule applies here. Love, respect, help, and protect yourself at all costs. Nobody will do this like you will do for yourself, NOR can anyone else do this for you. It comes from within you and therefore must be protected and uplifted by YOU.

In the end, it doesn't matter if love comes to you in the form of one of the categories above, your beloved pet, God/whoever you pray to. Just know this —being centered in love makes you powerful. And above all else:

Leaders full of love lead differently and better.

Self-Reflection Challenge:
1. Think of a time you were dealing with a toxic relationship (of any kind) and you were also responsible for leading an important initiative. Were you at your best? Was your performance impacted in any way because of the toxic relationship?
2. We can always devote more time to self-love related activities. What are some things you can reasonably do over the next ninety days to ensure you dedicate time to love on yourself? Write them down and make sure you implement a strategy to see them through.
3. When you are in need of support from others, do you have a safety net of individuals that you can depend on? When they need the same from you, are you equally available? Make sure the support is balanced. Sometimes, people give more than they receive. In some instances that is okay, but as with all things balance is important.

Chapter 19: Positioning

1. Do you have to always be in charge?
2. Do you feel the need to be center stage?
3. Do you feel as though you always should be credited for work you were involved in?
4. Do you promote the work of others?
5. Do you seek out opportunities for other people to have the limelight?
6. Do you invest any of your time in helping build an emerging leader?
7. Do you look for talent in people that is not previously known to you?
8. Are you okay being in the background while others on your team are applauded?

<u>Here is the answer sheet for the above</u>:
1. Do you have to always be in charge?
 Leaders need to also know how to follow.

2. Do you feel the need to be center stage?
You can be a "Leader Diva," but you have to share the stage (and sometimes not even step on the stage) in order to lead.

3. Do you promote the work of others?
I hope so, you have to be good at being someone else's hype woman sometimes.

4. Do you seek out opportunities for other people to have the limelight?
"As much as possible," should be your response.

5. Do you invest any of your time in helping build an emerging leader?
Lord, please answer this with a resounding "YES!"

6. Do you look for talent in people that is not previously known to you?

I hope so as you will not have the answers or solutions working as a team of one.

7. Are you okay being in the background while others on your team are applauded?
Yes, and you should be the person clapping the loudest.

I usually end with self-reflection questions, but this time we are starting with them! Positioning is about being able to be flexible and play a variety of positions on a team. I like to use a football team example. Sometimes as a leader of anything, you play the role of the football commissioner, sometimes the team owner, other times the quarterback, sometimes the kicker and other times a wide receiver. An effective leader understands that sometimes the role they are playing has to be adjusted in order to achieve ultimate success. You have to be okay with the fact that sometimes the best solution doesn't come from you, nor should that always be the case.

Sometimes, your best move is scoping out talent and hiring people that bring special skill sets to the team or table. That is the role you play, and you are comfortable seeking out input and trusting the solutions presented by other talented people. It's looking around at a team of people and engaging with them in a way that makes them comfortable offering up an opinion without feeling like it will just be shut down anyway. I have heard a million stories over the years of people being angry at someone in a leadership role for taking credit for an idea that was theirs. They presented it to the leader, the leader made no indication of whether they thought the idea was good or not yet, turned around and made it seem as though they came up with the idea on their own. This has happened to probably all of us at some point in time. Having been on the receiving end of this before, I am probably oversensitive about this and try to make sure I give credit where credit is due!

The most effective leaders that I have had the pleasure of learning from always emphasized the fundamental concept of teamwork. That's what this boils down to. Can you truly be a team player and have the flexibility to work whatever position is required at the moment? A leader who believes it is their job to go in a corner alone and come back out with all of the answers is doomed to fail. Sure, you should have the ability to think critically and come up with solutions to problems you have identified. However, the difference is, you know your solution is subject to change with input from the team and you are absolutely okay with this.

Many would-be great leaders struggle with this concept. It is easy in philosophy but not so much so in actual practice. Your idea may be one of the best, but you have to leave room for input from a team to make sure all of your blind spots are covered.

This is what positioning is really about. If you grasp the basic concept of how important it is to team with others and use your skill sets to find solutions to tough problems, you will be more effective as a leader. No one wants to work with *or* for someone who presents as though they have all the answers. Why would they? *If you already know everything, then why do you need me? What value do I have?* These are perfectly legitimate questions for someone working for a leader to ask.

Positioning requires you to step out of your own shoes so you can literally see the situation from all angles. In order to do that, you have to be comfortable easing into different roles that may not always look like the exact definition of what you imagine a leader is. It is an artful ability to flow in and out of a variety of positions and take in multiple perspectives at any given time. It is a task, but necessary to have longevity as an effective leader.

Be the leader that has enough humility and confidence to know when to fall back, follow someone else's lead and be comfortable sitting in another chair besides the head of the table.

Now, reflect back on the questions posed at the start of the chapter for self-reflection about the type of leader you really are and what you hope to be.

Chapter 20: Be Fabulous

Passionate
Ambitious
Confident
Graceful
Radiant
Badass
Bold
Real

These are the immediate words that come to mind when I think about what it means to be FABULOUS. I have spent this time with you sharing lessons that I have learned about being a good, effective woman leader. It is only fitting that I end our dialogue with this, simply: However you implement any of the concepts that I have shared, you must remember to do it in a way that is full of fabulousness! Pull out a sticky note pad and write each of the above words down as they all perfectly define what it means to be a fabulous leader. Place the notes in a place where you can access them on demand. Being fabulous while you are slaying dragons is the part that distinguishes you from men leaders. You get to do this with a flare that is unique to women leaders. Oh, how fun it is to be all the things in this book and get to do it in the best shoes and flawless spirit of confidence and grace in a way that only a WOMAN can do.

You have to define what fabulous means for you. It's not necessarily a well-made-up, flawless face; the best hair style; or the best shoes. (You see the shoe theme here?) It is how you display and exude an unforgettable essence. When you are in the room, you command attention. You don't have to be loud to be heard, and you don't have to have on bright colors to be seen. But make no mistake about it, when you enter any room, meeting, or other occasion, your presence is known and it is missed when you are gone. That is what being fabulous means to me.

This concept of being fabulous comes from within yourself. All of the lessons that we have discussed in this book come together like a puzzle and, if used correctly, help you be a fabulous, effective leader. Don't be afraid to own your confidence. Sit, walk, and talk like you are the business because feeling the part is half the battle! When I set out to write this book, I didn't know how I would translate my workshops into an actual book. What kept me going when life got in the way was the feeling that I had some secrets to share that would be someone's key to success. I hope that this journey has left you as what I hoped in the beginning you would be:

1. Empowered
2. Inspired
3. Motivated
4. Badass

I don't proclaim to know everything, but I know that the lessons I have shared with you in this book have helped me thrive as a woman leader. This framework is not a one size fits all. We each have different life experiences and perspectives. It is my hope that you are able to take these concepts and apply them in a way that works for who you uniquely are.

I would fail miserably as a leader if I didn't find an opportunity to share and spread these lessons with other women. If you are reading this book, then **congratulations** on choosing to invest in yourself. Learning and growing is a forever thing. Taking the time to reset, learn new concepts, or practice concepts you already are familiar with but have not been able to focus on requires dedication. A commitment to being a change agent or making an impact in the world. I believe we are facing a leadership crisis at key positions in our country and even across the world. I hope you are inspired to go out and be the leader that helps to bring humility, strength, courage and intellect back to our world. I hope you step out and lead in a way that women are uniquely positioned to do. I am rooting for you! We need you girlfriend, so let's shake things up a bit.

In the end, I want to look back over my life and know that I did the best I could with the strengths that were provided to me. I didn't choose to be a leader; it chose me and I accepted the lifelong task. I am happy to fulfill what this mission holds for me.

Who would have thought that the pre-K three-year-old that started out on a path of learning forty-two years ago would have the nerve to write this book? Certainly not me, but this is what happens when a woman **decides to LEAD**. I hope I have made that little girl's dreams come true.

Finally, to all of you phenomenal women who went on this journey with me. **<u>Thank you</u>** for engaging with me and talking to me in your head for this ride. I had a blast and I am filled with gratitude that you chose me and stayed with me to the end. Go and be badass. Much gratitude

– MJ

Acknowledgments

Whew! I did it!! One day this will soak in, but right now, I just want to thank several people who have helped make this book happen.

First, I thank my husband Richard Johnson, who has read chapters, encouraged me to keep going and believes in me the way that only he can. He listens to me even when I think he is not and I think he is even using some of the strategies from this book (see it CAN apply to anyone)! Richard is a constant support for me and I am forever grateful that the universe saw fit to bring us back together at this particular point in time. I love you and would not have been able to do any of this without your love and support.

I thank my Dad, Joseph Saxby, who is one of the most important people in my life and always has been. He gifted me with his talents as a speaker and a writer. He encourages me and made sure I stayed the course. He is a critic and a fan all wrapped into one. I also learned that he is a real-life warrior and I am honored that I was chosen to be his daughter.

For every friend in my circle that supported this effort in a variety of ways, I thank you all. Soo many friends showed their support and encouraged me in their own way, and I am grateful for the love and support from each of you.

Karen Knox is my editor and I will be eternally grateful that we connected. This experience was scary and it got scarier once I submitted this manuscript to a stranger to review and polish it. She made the process seamless and I hope this is the start of many things to come. Thank you, Karen!

Thanks to my photographer, Trey Langston! Trey provided the photography on the covers of the book. I do **not** wake up looking like the pictures on this book cover, but he got me together! Thank you, Ericka & Erin Robinson, for the book cover design work and **all** the revisions that I am sure drove you nuts! Thanks for hanging with me.

Finally, last but not least, thank you to every single leader that I have had the pleasure of working with over the years. I have experienced such a wide range of examples of what good leadership looks like and have learned from the cream of the crop. If you played any role in teaching me and coaching me, or played ANY part in me being the leader I am, THANK YOU. My favorite leaders know who they are and I hope I am making you proud. Forever grateful.

Conversations with Monica

Interested in continuing the dialogue with Monica regarding becoming an effective, fabulous woman leader? Please connect with Monica on Twitter at @mojohnsonspeaks or https://twitter.com/mojohnsonspeaks

Interested in booking Monica for a Fab 30 workshop? Please visit www.monicasjohnson.com/ to contact Monica regarding booking a workshop or for media inquiries. Be sure to subscribe to the website so you can be informed of *Fab 30* future events.

Interested in reaching out to Monica directly about the book? Please reach out via the contact page on the website.

Thank you!